GRANNY'S
NATURAL
REMEDIES

GRANNY'S NATURAL REMEDIES

Traditional Cures for Everyday Ailments

BRENDA EVANS

canary
press

ISBN: 978-0-9562655-2-4

Printed and bound in India

10 9 8 7 6 5 4 3 2 1

Cover by Anthony Prudente
Internal design by Vivian Foster
Illustrations by Tegan J. Humphryes

Contents

Down Memory Lane

Cover up your coughs and sneezes,
If you don't, you'll spread diseases.

Being a granny myself, I am often hit by a wave of nostalgia, musing on all those moments in my life when my own 'Tiny Gran' (named because she was only 4 ft 8 in tall) came to my rescue. Once a year my sister and I were packed into the car surrounded with endless bags and the family dog, Kimmy, and driven down to North Devon to my grandparents' home in an idyllic rural setting. Neither of us travelled particularly well, so mother always made sure she carried a Thermos flask filled with ginger tea to try and alleviate the feelings of nausea. I can still taste the sweet, amber liquid to this day and it is something I used on my own children and now my grandchildren. My daughter is a great believer in natural medicine and is always asking me if I have any magical remedies if, say, her son falls over and scrapes his knee or comes to her with a tummy ache. Over the years I have written down numerous natural remedies which have been handed down to me through the various generations.

I have deviated slightly in my story, nothing unusual when you reach the twilight years. My grandparents lived in a tiny thatched, whitewashed cottage, with a living room, a kitchen of sorts and two rooms up a very steep flight of stairs. There was no running water – only a pump in the back garden – no electricity and no gas, so their life was tough but happy. None of this 'keeping up with the Joneses' for them, they were content with their lot and asked for nothing.

As adolescents, my sister and I found our holidays in North Devon an adventure, and accompanying grandad to the allotment to feed his chickens was the highlight of my mornings. As a young child, the word 'allotment' meant nothing to me, so I would run down the creaky old stairs yelling, 'Chickies up top! Chickies up top!' until my grandad allowed me to bury my hands deep into the bowl of scraps that were to be used as chicken feed. It was a pleasant smell that remains in my nostrils even today whenever I cast my mind back.

Avian vets had not been 'invented' and the likes of modern antibiotics and premixed medicated poultry food were unheard of. Grandad relied on his own tried and tested cures to keep his flock in tip-top condition and I don't remember – apart from those he culled for the table – any of his chickens having to be destroyed due to ill health. With his help and a host of garden grubs, 'Chickies up top' were a happy feathered family.

The Ants' Nest

One of my earliest memories of my granny coming to my rescue was the time my sister and I were sitting beside a lavender hedge in the front garden. The garden was raised and we could see the world go by from there. My sister, who was six years older, was reading *Alice's Adventures in Wonderland* to me – my favourite story as a young child and indeed now. I was looking at the beautiful drawings and listening intently, unaware that my bottom was lunch to a host of ants. I was aware of a pricking sensation, but I was too absorbed by the story to do anything about it other than have the odd scratch. It was my sister who jumped up and started running round the garden like a mad thing. Unbeknown to us we had sat right on top of an ants' nest and they were trying to let us know that we were not welcome.

We both ran indoors screaming, clutching our behinds. Granny made us bend over, pull down our panties, and unceremoniously expose our rear ends. I remember her muttering, 'Oh dear . . . oh dear

. . . oh dear', and rushing off to her larder telling us to stay exactly where we were. She came back carrying a small white bowl and a white handkerchief and then proceeded to spread a white paste all over our bottoms which, I remember vividly, took the sting out within seconds. At the time I had no reason to ask her what was in the little white bowl, but in later years I discovered it was a simple paste of bicarbonate of soda and water liberally applied to our rather red backsides. This is a true and tested remedy I have used time and time again to calm down insect bites.

Keeping the Candle Burning

Bedtime was a challenge at granny's house. Without the luxury of electricity, the cottage was lit by small oil lamps hung from various hooks around the walls and one central one on the living room table. Just negotiating the stairs was an amazing achievement when your legs were short, but climbing them with a candle in one hand was difficult to say the least. Granny always made her own candles from the beeswax collected from the two hives at the bottom of the garden. Although they worked efficiently, she frequently made them too fat for my podgy little hands to grasp, so two hands were needed. This made the task of going to bed even harder, as you really needed one free hand to shield the flame against draughts. My sister and I would have bets as to whether we could get to the top without the flame going out, or dripping blobs of candlewax on the stair treads. I remember one particularly windy night and I was on my third attempt to reach the top of what seemed an endless flight of stairs. Each time the flame blew out I had to return to the room below and ask granny to relight it with a wax taper she kept by the back door. We were forbidden from putting the taper in the fire ourselves because she was scared we would get burned.

The third attempt was successful and I was so excited that I forgot myself and turned round to see if my sister was behind me. As I turned round I tipped the candle, and some hot wax ran down my bare arm. I screamed in pain, dropping the candle in the process, nearly causing a fire as the flame scorched the wood at the top of the stairs. Granny was out of her chair, knitting needles flying everywhere, and climbing the stairs as fast as her arthritic body would carry her. She picked me up in her arms, which was a mammoth task considering her small stature, and sat me on the edge of the bed. She stroked my hair and wiped my tears away and then vanished downstairs, telling me to stay there until she returned. She came back with a bowl of milk and proceeded to bathe my arm very gently. After about five minutes, the pain was starting to subside. Then she fetched a prickly looking leaf in her hand which was oozing some kind of greenish gel. She rubbed it on my arm and then tucked me up into bed. I remember she left me a saucer with a little of the gel on it and she said that I should rub some more on in the night if the burning got too bad.

Before finally saying goodnight, granny went downstairs and got the dented old warming pan which contained hot coals, and rubbed it over my inner sheet. This was usually reserved for the grown-ups, but because I had had a nasty accident, I was given a special treat that night. As I pulled the blankets up, I coaxed granny's fat ginger cat, Maximilian, to come and sleep at the foot of my bed. I can tell you he didn't need much encouragement and we shared each other's warmth for the rest of the night.

Needless to say I didn't need to add any more of the magic green gel, I slept like a baby – granny's remedy had worked wonders again. The green plant turned out to be aloe vera, which I have used for many things since, once I learned of its invaluable properties.

I have many things to thank my granny for – precious memories, tenderness, and miraculous cures for numerous ailments – to name but a few. I, in turn, have attempted to pass these down to my own family and I am proud to say that both my daughter and son would rather try some form of natural remedy than rush off down to the chemist for a proprietary alternative. Of course, common sense has to prevail; if you know the symptoms are serious then you must always seek medical advice. The natural remedies in this book are only designed to help you with minor problems, but I think you will find they are ones that you will use time and time again.

I hope you enjoy the journey through this book, with little snippets of my own life to give you some light reading on the way.

Chapter One

Old Wives' Tales

Old Wives' Tales

True or false, I hear you say
Can an apple a day keep the doctor away?
Is a black cat a sign of good luck
Or just a myth that has stuck?

Having joined the ranks of the septuagenarians recently, I have many years of memories that I can reflect on. Many of those spent as a child involved endless instructions from my own mother and granny telling me that doing 'this' and doing 'that' would be bad for my health. Some of these things can be described as old wives' tales with not an element of truth behind them, while others made a modicum of sense. Whether or not they are true really doesn't matter, they are just a reminder of what our ancestors used to say. Not all the ones mentioned are to do with natural remedies, but I thought they were fun anyway and a little part of social history that has almost been forgotten. Because I wanted to learn more about these so-called wives' tales, I decided to do a little research in my spare time to see which ones – if any – were actually based on fact. The deeper I delved the more the memories came flooding back. We were only allowed one bath a week in my childhood and that didn't usually last long because the bathroom was often too cold to hang around in. Mum would hang the towels in front of the fire to warm them, but that meant they had a slight aroma of woodsmoke to mingle with that of the coal tar soap. No luxuries for us to add to our bathwater, like ylang ylang to make you sleep or ginseng and ginger to improve the circulation!

Bathtime at granny's was no better, although she did put the tin bath in front of the fire which meant we had a warm glow. However, being the younger of the two sisters I always had to go last and the water was scummy and lukewarm by the time I got in. If we had our bath early before tea was ready we used to ask if we could go out to play for a while. Granny always said, 'You can't go out with your hair wet, you'll catch your death!' As a five-year-old, this was threatening talk and I used to get a book and sit by the fire until my hair was dry. My sister, being older and wiser, used to ignore the ramblings of a senior citizen and go out anyway. I always used to have visions of her shivering and coughing until there was no life left in her body. Of course that never happened and I don't even remember her ever having caught a cold from going outside with wet hair.

I hope you find this as interesting as I did. As I started to read more and more about the things our ancestors used to say, I discovered that there is a bit of truth behind some of these old sayings.

An apple a day keeps the doctor away

This saying was frequently used as an encouragement to children to eat more fruit. There were none of the exotic fruits that are available today, so apples were part of the staple diet, many coming from the family's own garden. There is a small amount of truth behind this saying, as apples, like many fruits, contain components that are beneficial to our health, reducing the chance of heart disease, strokes, and cancer just as examples. The skin is as beneficial as the flesh of the apple, so it is important to remember to eat both. Apples can definitely help to lower the level of 'bad' cholesterol and, by eating two each day, you can reduce it by as much as 16 per cent. They are also believed to be beneficial for women of menopausal age, as they can help increase bone density, lessening the chances of osteoporosis. Apple juice drunk on a regular basis can also be beneficial for children who suffer from asthma, so it is worth encouraging your children to drink fresh fruit juice rather than sodas, many of which are loaded with sugars and artificial colourings.

Feed a cold and starve a fever

This really is an old wives' tale; denying your body food during any type of illness means it is not getting all the necessary nutrients it needs to get well. It is vital to make sure you drink plenty of fluids if you have either a cold or flu, to replace those lost through the illness. Our bodies have sufficient reserves to last three days without any ill effects, but any longer than that is not recommended. In fact the original phrase, before someone misquoted it, was 'Feed a cold, STAVE [*to ward off*] a fever' – not quite the same thing at all!

Don't walk with bare feet

Parents and grandparents have been telling their children for eons not to walk with bare feet or they will get worms. The origin of this old wives' tale is uncertain, but that is all it is. Although there may be other dangers to children running round with bare feet, such as cutting their feet on sharp objects or stubbing their toes, they certainly won't get worms from doing so.

Getting out of bed on the wrong side will bring bad luck

According to superstition, the wrong side of the bed is the left-hand side, and this is something that can be dated back to the Romans. If people were grumpy or surly they were said to have 'got out of bed on the wrong side'. Of course there was no truth behind this whatsoever, other than a simple superstition about the 'left' in general. Romans believed you should never put your left shoe on before your right or walk into a house with your left foot first. If you are going to have a bad day, you will have it regardless of what side of the bed you climb out of.

Catching a baby cold

This old wives' tale goes back centuries to when it was believed that a woman should never go out in the rain if she had just given birth to a baby or she would 'catch a baby cold'. A new mother would always be accompanied by a friend or member of the family for weeks after giving birth, just to make sure she never got caught in the rain. This old superstition probably arose from the fact that many women died shortly after childbirth due to unsanitary conditions or excessive blood loss; it certainly wasn't anything to do with going out in a sudden downpour, though.

Dandelions

There are two old wives' tales regarding dandelions, the first of which I am sure many people of my age have heard time and time again. Granny always used to say if you pick, smell or even come in contact with a dandelion in the late afternoon you will wet the bed at night. We all know that dandelions cannot make us wet the bed, but did you know they could actually be a contributory factor? Dandelions are in fact diuretic, and a diuretic increases the amount of urine that is released by the body. However, for this to have any effect you would certainly need to do more than smell a dandelion or come in contact with it, you would need to eat it. I can't imagine anyone sitting down to enjoy a meal of dandelions, so the chances of your child wetting the bed because of this plant are negligible.

The second myth surrounding dandelions – and that is all it is – is that you can tell how many years you have left to live by blowing on the head of a dandelion that has gone to seed. It is rumoured that you will live as many years as the number of seeds left on the head. Treat it as the old wives' tale that it is, and you and your grandchildren can have fun playing the game.

Don't cross your eyes or they will stay that way

How many times did you hear your parents say that when you were pulling a funny face? Of course most of us have pulled silly faces or crossed our eyes to see how silly we can look at some time or another. I suspect the saying came out of embarrassment on the part of the parents when their child was behaving oddly in front of strangers. No one knows where this saying started, but you can be certain it doesn't contain any validity.

Morning sickness – you are having a girl

There are numerous old wives' tales that surround pregnancy and what sex the baby is going to be. One of the more common myths is that if you suffer from morning sickness, then you are going to have a girl. There is not an ounce of truth in this saying, it is merely the hormones released during pregnancy that cause morning sickness and these hormones will be released whether the baby is a boy or a girl. Some women are more prone to morning sickness than others, but midwives' used to use this as a comfort to those women who were suffering the most.

Also worth mentioning while on the subject of pregnancy is the myth that if you are carrying your baby round the front then you are having a girl, or extra weight on the hips and bottom means that it is a boy. Again there is no truth to this whatsoever, it depends on the shape of the woman's torso. If a woman is very short in the torso, then there is no other place for her to show than in the front. Mind you, this old saying was fun and kept you guessing; nowadays most parents opt to find out the sex of their unborn baby with the help of modern technology.

Eat up your carrots and you will see in the dark

Even the modern generation has heard this saying, although to most it just sounds like a way of getting children to eat their vegetables. In fact, this saying does have a small amount of truth behind it. Carrots contain large amounts of beta-carotene which the body is able to transform into vitamin A. Vitamin A is then turned into a protein called rhodospin which is found in the part of the retina that is sensitive to light. The British used this old wives' tale during World

War II, saying that their soldiers were fed on carrots to help them see enemy planes better. Of course it was a twisting of the truth to try and keep the real reason – radar – a tactical secret.

If a mirror breaks there will be a death in the house

This is another superstition that is commonly known, but the original old wives' tale was that if the mirror fell off the wall by itself there would be a death in the house. No one knows where this story came from and although there can be no guarantee that someone won't die if a mirror falls off a wall, I would imagine it would be nothing more than a coincidence. It could possibly scare you to death, I suppose, if you believe in poltergeists!

The other belief is that if you break a mirror you will receive seven years of bad luck. This old wives' tale can be traced back to the Romans, who were the first people to create glass mirrors. They believed that a person's soul was trapped inside the mirror and that by breaking the glass, the soul would be broken too. Because they believed it took seven years for the soul to be restored to normal, it was thought the person who broke the mirror would have one long string of unfortunate events since he or she no longer had a healthy soul to ward off any evil spirits. My suggestion is to avoid breaking a mirror at all costs as it is not worth finding out if your soul will take the seven years to recover.

Here comes the bride

Many people still adhere to the old superstition that it is unlucky for the groom to see the bride in her wedding dress before she walks down the aisle, or see the wedding dress until the day of the wedding. Legend says that if the groom does either of these, the couple will experience bad luck and it will lead to a failure in the marriage. I am sure many happily married couples will tell you that this is just an old wives' tale and that they have been happily married for many years despite disregarding this superstition. However, on my part, I think it is rather nice if the groom does not see his bride in all her finery until the big day.

Eat up your crusts

How many of you were told to eat your crusts when you were children. Girls were usually told that it would make their hair curl, while boys were told it would put hair on their chests. Neither of these are true of course, it was much more likely that during the war our parents were encouraging us not to waste food. Quite where this saying comes from, no one really knows – perhaps there was a little girl with very curly hair somewhere who always finished her crusts!

The Midas touch

This saying refers to someone who seems to make a success of everything they undertake and it can be traced back to a story regarding King Midas, ruler of Phrygia (modern-day Turkey). Some of Midas's servants were working the fields when they noticed a creature that was half-man/half-goat asleep in the king's vineyard. The men captured the creature and took it to their king believing that he would be impressed with their find. The king, however, recognized the creature to be the satyr Silenus, an assistant to the god Dionysus. He was displeased that they should have treated the satyr in such a manner and ordered his men to release it immediately. Silenus was so thankful to Midas for treating him with respect that when he returned home he told his god what had happened and Dionysus granted Midas one wish. Midas asked that everything he touched should turn to gold. Dionysus was doubtful about granting such a wish, but he kept his promise to Midas. Midas was thrilled as everything he touched turned to gold as Dionysus had promised. Delighted he rushed to tell his daughter, but as he took her by the hand she turned into a statue of gold. Midas fled back to the god and begged him to remove his special power. Dionysus allowed Midas to wash his hands in the Pactolus river to wash away the special power and everything was returned to normal.

A watched pot never boils

Many old wives' tales seem to be to do with the kitchen, but that is probably because this is where the women spent most of their time. Many cooks don't like to watch a pot on the cooker because they believe it will take much longer to come to the boil. There is, of course, no truth to this, it just seems a lot longer because you are concentrating on one thing and not doing something else to take your mind off it.

Lucky New Year's Eve

There is a very old saying that if the first person to enter your home after the clock strikes twelve on New Year's Eve is a tall dark-haired man, then you will be blessed with luck in the new year. Although there is no way of tracing the origin of this old saying, to be on the safe side maybe you should invite some good looking men over to help you celebrate.

If a black cat crosses your path

There is an old wives' tale that says if a black cat crosses your path it will bring you good luck and fortune. Although this is a nice one to believe, the tale is likely rooted in early Christianity. People who had black cats were generally associated with witchcraft. Cats can be spooky creatures so why not believe in this one and see if good luck comes your way. Variations of this tale say that you must politely greet the cat or alternatively stroke the cat three times to make sure you have good luck.

There is another belief that if a black cat crosses your path you will have bad luck, but I guess that depends on what happens to you the first time you see one. If you are too busy looking at the cat and you twist your ankle falling down the kerb, then you may be a believer of the latter.

Throwing the bridal bouquet

At weddings it is quite common for the bride to stand in front of a group of her single friends and, with her back to them, toss her bouquet over her head. It is believed that the person who catches the bouquet will be the next one to get married. Once again this is a nice tradition and one that probably gives a few single girls hope, but in truth it dates to a time in England when people who came across a wedding would run after the bride and tear pieces from her dress and bouquet so they could take a part of her happiness. To try and keep the scavengers at bay, the bride would throw her bouquet over her shoulder in the hope they would stop and pick it up.

Putting butter on a burn

I remember as a child burning my finger while toasting crumpets with my sister. The first thing my mother did was to rush to the kitchen and get the butter to spread on my burn. It did nothing to alleviate the pain, but then my mother always listened to old wives' tales. The real truth is that putting butter, or indeed anything greasy, on a burn is definitely not the thing to do. The grease will actually hold the heat, causing the burning sensation to increase.

Don't give cut flowers to the sick

There are many old wives' tales regarding illness and even death, but one that has stuck with me is that you shouldn't give cut flowers to anyone who is unwell. The old belief was that the flowers would suck all the oxygen out of the air and cause the sick person's demise. Luckily this is a very old and inaccurate story, but if you want to be on the safe side you can always just send a bunch of grapes!

Cutting the cake

This isn't really an old wives' tale, just a lovely tradition which is still carried on at modern wedding ceremonies, whereby the couple will cut the first slice of the wedding cake and then make a wish. This tradition dates back to when Charles II was king of England. The baker would be asked to design a cake which usually had many layers. The top layer always represented the new husband and wife and the love they shared for each other. After the ceremony, the cake would be broken over the bride's head to bring her good luck and fertility.

Don't lie!

'Don't tell lies or you will get a pimple on your tongue!' This has been used by many a parent when they have found out their child has told a little white lie. Of course it isn't true, but to a child just the threat of something like that is enough to make them tell the truth. Pimples on the tongue can be caused simply by biting the tongue or by various viruses. In a roundabout way it could be true, because the stress from telling a white lie might lead you to have a pimple on the tongue, so it is probably better not to take the chance.

Don't swallow your chewing gum

I remember being really frightened when I was quite young by my mother telling me that if I swallowed my chewing gum it would stick to my ribs. It made me stop eating gum but I later found out there wasn't an iota of truth in her old wives' tale. Just like everything else you swallow, gum will go straight into your stomach and get digested. It will certainly not stick to anything on the way down!

A lucky four-leaf clover

The four-leaf clover has been a popular symbol of luck for many centuries. It is mostly associated with Ireland where the three-leaf clover is said to represent the Holy Trinity – one leaf for the Father, one for the Son and one for the Holy Spirit. If you are lucky enough to find one with four leaves, then the fourth represents God's Grace and will give the finder hope, faith, love, and luck throughout his or her future life. If you go way back in history, Eve is thought to have carried a four-leaf clover from the Garden of Eden.

Unlucky Friday the 13th

This must be one of the most common myths around today, that Friday the 13th is a day of bad luck and misfortune. Some people actually have a phobia regarding this day – paraskevidekatriaphobia – and will not even leave their house. There are many ancient myths regarding Friday the 13th, but the most common belief dates back to Friday, 13 October 1307. On this day the Pope and King Philip IV of France issued a secret death warrant against the Templar Knights. Despite leading exemplary lives within the Church, the knights were deemed to be heretics and their power was removed. Their Grand Master, Jacques DeMolay, was arrested and subsequently tortured before being crucified. From then on Friday the 13th has always been associated with bad luck. Because there will always be something bad that happens on Friday the 13th somewhere in the world, this is going to be an old wives' tale that will be handed down from generation to generation.

Don't dress her in black

Another old wives' tale associated with death, says that if a woman is buried in black she will come back to haunt her family. Many families today still believe this superstition and will purchase something new for their loved one to be buried in. This superstition comes down to what the individual believes, but I suggest that you don't do anything to upset your relative while she is alive and then she will have no reason to haunt you.

An itchy palm means money

According to the old wives' tale, if the palm on your right hand starts to itch, then you will receive some money. However, if you scratch it, you will stop the money from coming. The reverse is said to apply to the left hand; this foretells that you will be paying out money. Many people still believe in this tale and it is another one that has been handed down through the generations. Is it true? I doubt that it has anything to do with money, but you should refrain from scratching your right palm when it itches just in case . . .

Little white lies

I am certain everyone has heard this one but I don't imagine you know the origin behind it. It was another way of parents warning their children about the consequences of lying by saying that every time they told a fib they would get a little white mark on their fingernail. For most young children this would be enough to make them tell the truth, but of course those little white marks are nothing to do with lying. They are usually the result of some trauma to the nail itself, perhaps by shutting it in a drawer or something similar. Mind you, I think I will still keep using this old saying because it works wonders.

If your ears are burning

There is an old wives' tale that says if your ears are burning then someone is talking about you. Some people add a further dimension to this myth, believing that you can tell if a person is saying good or bad things about you. It is said that if the left ear is burning good things are being said and if the right ear, then bad things are being said. It was originally used by mothers to discourage their children from gossiping and perhaps the burning came from a good clip round the ear! How can you be sure, though, that the next time one of your ears is burning that you are not the topic of conversation somewhere?

Wishing on a star

This is a wonderful old wives' tale and a great way for your children to make a wish. The first star that you see in the sky at night will make your wish come true if you say:

Starlight, star bright, first star I see tonight.
I wish I may, I wish I might, have the wish I wish tonight.

This has been used for generations and it is worth keeping it going just to see the look on the face of a child who thinks its wish will come true. Who are we to say whether this is true or not?

Don't go swimming after eating

I can't remember how many times my mother told me to wait an hour before going swimming if I had just had lunch. I believed her totally that I would get stomach cramps and drown if I didn't wait at least one hour. There is no medical proof that eating causes cramps while swimming, although it probably isn't a good idea to let your child go in the water if they have just eaten a big meal. A sandwich or a light snack will have no ill effects at all. This is just an ancient belief that has been spun totally out of proportion.

Stealing a baby's breath

For hundreds of years people believed that if they had a cat in the house when a new baby arrived, it would lay on the baby and steal its breath. This forced many couples to get rid of a beloved family pet just before bringing the new arrival home. This old wives' tale has been around since the days when witches were feared, but in truth the myth holds no weight at all. Of course, you should never leave animals and babies unsupervised; it is possible your cat might seek warmth by laying with the baby and unintentionally leave it short of breath. Just watch carefully and make sure they don't snuggle up too closely.

Lucky horseshoe

The horseshoe is considered very lucky and used to be hung in many homes to protect and attract good fortune for the family who lived there. There are many reasons why it is believed that a horseshoe can bring luck and here are just a few:

- There are usually seven nail holes in a horseshoe and the number seven is considered to be lucky.
- Horseshoes are made by blacksmiths who, by tradition, are considered to be lucky.
- A witch is unable to walk under a horseshoe.
- A horseshoe in your bedroom will keep nightmares at bay.

Don't touch that toad

Many people believed that if you touched a toad you would get a wart. It is easy to see why people thought this to be true, as a toad is covered in many bumps and warts. However, warts on a human are caused by a virus and cannot possibly be passed on by a toad. This probably came about because some toads look a little scary and your mother was trying to discourage you from touching them.

You'll know when someone is thinking of you

There is an old wives' tale that says someone is thinking of you romantically every time you get hiccups. Although that would be nice to believe, a hiccup is merely a spasm of the diaphragm. There is a variant on this myth that says if a woman has hiccups on the night before her wedding then a past love is thinking of her. I am one person who would like to go on believing this saying and my children like to believe it, too.

The wishing well

According to a well-known old wives' tale, to throw a penny into a wishing well will bring good luck. As the penny hits the water the thrower should make his or her wish and, as long as they don't share it with anyone else, the wish is said to come true. Although the exact origins of the practice are not known, offering money to water is an old tradition that can be dated back to the Romans and also Celtic mythology. One of the oldest examples of a wishing well in Britain is that located on the north-eastern tip of England. This discovery unearthed about 16,000 coins, some even dating back to the fifth century. I know I can't pass a wishing well without throwing a coin in the water – well you don't really know whether your wishes will come true or not do you, and I am not prepared to take the chance.

Pulling the wishbone

I remember every Christmas hooking my little finger round one end of the wishbone from our turkey, while my sister did the same on the other side. They say that the person who ends up with the longer half can wish for something nice. Usually the bone was so slippery it was difficult to keep hold of, but I know that if I was the one lucky enough to get the longest bit I would wish for the perfect Christmas present. You see, we didn't open our presents until after lunch!

Don't put new shoes on the table

My mother always used to tell me off if I came home with a bag containing new shoes and left it on the table in the kitchen. She told me it would bring me bad luck but never knew the reason why. In olden days it was considered a sign of disrespect to put shoes on the table, purely because you shouldn't put anything dirty on a place where you eat. Another reason could be that to prepare dead people for their long journey to heaven, a pair of new shoes was placed on the corpse before it was put in the coffin. Also, did you know that if your new shoes squeak, it means you haven't paid for them!

Chapter Two

Granny's
Store Cupboard

Old Mother Hubbard

Old Mother Hubbard
Went to the cupboard
To get her poor doggie a bone,
When she got there
The cupboard was bare
So the poor little doggie had none.

When I mention my granny's kitchen, it wasn't the type of kitchen you would see in a modern home; it was a small room off the living room, which contained hooks for hanging preserved meat and dried herbs and this enormous walk-in larder. The shelves of the larder were stocked with rows of jars full of preserves my granny had lovingly prepared from fruit and vegetables grown in their garden and on the allotment on the other side of the hedge. There were bottles of vinegar, small packets containing powders like bicarbonate of soda and always a wooden bowl full of lemons. The strong smell of lavender still fills my nostrils, every time I mentally step into that larder, as grandma always had a few bunches hanging from the top shelf. Many items were still rationed after World War II, so everything in granny's larder was precious and *nothing* was ever wasted.

I will try and recall all the natural little miracles that granny kept in her store cupboard and give you a brief outline of their benefits in this chapter. I will go into more detail regarding the actual recipes and methods of treatment as you continue your journey through this book.

Nature's Own Medicine Cabinet

GARLIC (*Allium sativum*)
Having grown up in a family that loved gardening, I was used to seeing cloves of garlic sitting on the shelves of the kitchen cupboard. Little did I know then, the wonders of this tiny little herb from the onion family. The natural healing powers of this remarkable herb are quite simply amazing, and it has been performing miracles throughout the world for hundreds of years. Even some of the world's oldest civilizations believed garlic to be beneficial to good health. Egyptians, Hebrews, Greeks, and Romans all used it in their food, drinks, and as a medicine.

The Latin name *Allium* is derived from the Celtic word meaning hot, pungent, and burning, properties which are common to all the *Allium* species. It is certainly one of the earliest crops to be cultivated and continues to be grown extensively, even today, for both culinary and medicinal purposes.

It is the bulb of the plant that is used medicinally. When whole, the bulb has no odour, but as soon as it is cut or crushed it releases its characteristic pungent smell. Medicine men and physicians since time immemorial have sung its praises, and here is a list of many of the ailments it is believed to benefit if taken on a regular basis:

atherosclerosis, bites, blood clots, boils and cysts, calluses, cancer, cardiovascular disease, coughs, cold and influenza, corns, diabetes, diarrhoea, dysentery, earache, eczema, fatigue, food poisoning, fungus, heart attacks, haemorrhoids, high blood pressure, high cholesterol, hives, hypertension, immunodeficiency, infectious diseases, insect bites and stings, liver disease, pain, respiratory diseases, sclerosis, stress, toothache, warts, and worms.

Added to the above is the fact that garlic has antibiotic, antifungal, antiparasitic and antiviral properties. Taking all these things into consideration, it would be fair to say that having garlic and garlic oil in your store cupboard means you have one of the finest household remedies around, which is why it is first on my list.

Granny's Recipe for Garlic Oil

You will need
10 large garlic cloves, skinned and halved
570 ml (1 pint) olive oil (preferably extra virgin)
or sunflower oil

Method
1. Put the garlic into a warm, sterilized jar.
2. Heat the oil to around 180°C (350°F) and then pour it over the garlic in the jar and cover tightly.
3. Leave to stand in a sunny place for 1 to 2 weeks and then strain through two thicknesses of muslin.
4. Pour into a sterilized bottle and seal with a sterilized cork or screw-top.

Garlic oil is especially useful when treating infants and young children for earache, teething problems, nappy rash, athlete's foot, and minor burns. The oil needs to be kept refrigerated and a few drops of eucalyptus oil or vegetable glycerine will help to preserve it.

VINEGAR
Vinegar is an amazing product which was discovered by accident over 10,000 years ago and has been a staple ingredient of the British diet

ever since. I know that granny always had a bottle on her larder shelf and I would never be without it myself. Vinegar is a common element in cooking, but did you realize that it has many other uses as well, not only in natural cleaning but also in treating common ailments:

acne, age spots, arthritis, asthma, athlete's foot, body odour, bruises, burns, cancer prevention, cholesterol reduction, colds, constipation, corns and calluses, coughs, cramps, dandruff, diabetes, diarrhoea, digestion, ear infections, eczema, fatigue, flatulence, gout, haemorrhoids, headaches, heartburn, hiccups, insect bites and stings, insomnia, menstrual problems, morning sickness, muscle soreness, nail fungus, nappy rash, night sweats and hot flushes, nosebleed, osteoporosis, sinusitis, sore throat, sunburn, ulcers, urinary tract infection, varicose veins, warts, and yeast infection.

The favoured vinegar for general health is apple cider vinegar, because it absorbs all the natural goodness from the fruit, such as potassium, magnesium, calcium, iron, and phosphorus. It is a powerful detoxifying and purifying agent and can break down fatty deposits in the body. By destroying these deposits it can help in your general health by improving the function of vital organs such as the bladder, liver and kidneys. It can also assist in thinning the blood which helps in preventing high blood pressure. If you suffer from digestive problems, you might like to consider taking a mixture of apple cider vinegar and water before eating, as it seems to prevent diarrhoea and other digestive upsets. In fact, as you can see above, the list is endless and vinegar will crop up time and time again as you read through the other sections of this book. Of course please check with your doctor before making any drastic dietary changes.

If you are feeling adventurous, apple cider vinegar isn't too difficult to make. Here is my tried and tested recipe which my great grandmother scribbled down in an old notebook – which has been handed down through the family and, although rather tattered, is still in existence today.

Making your own apple cider vinegar

This recipe is ideal if you have an abundance of windfalls of sweet dessert apples. The sweeter the better as the higher sugar content will make a stronger cider which is better for fermentation. Do not use a metal container when making vinegar, because the acid in the mixture will corrode metal or aluminium.

Step 1

Thoroughly wash the apples and remove any badly bruised or damaged parts. Crush the apples into a pulp and strain off the juice through a piece of muslin or through a fine-mesh strainer. If you have the luxury of a juicer in your kitchen, then you can use this to extract the liquid.

Step 2

Now is the time to start the fermentation process. Pour all the apple juice into one or more containers (depending, of course, on the amount of juice you have extracted) until each container is two thirds full. A glass demijohn is perfect for this stage. Cover the jar with a piece of clean muslin and hold in place with an elastic band. Keep the jar away from direct sunlight in a place where you can keep a constant temperature of between 60 and 75°F (15 and 21°C to those of you who have successfully gone metric!). Make sure you stir the liquid every day to ensure you are incorporating enough oxygen into the liquid. These last two factors are very important to ensure that your vinegar is not contaminated. You should notice that the liquid is starting to smell a bit like vinegar after about three to four weeks. Using a clean spoon, taste each day until it reaches the tartness you like.

Step 3
Your vinegar is now ready to use. You will notice that there is a sediment in the bottom of the jar; this is an important part of the vinegar and should be stirred well before pouring the liquid into smaller bottles for storage. Make sure each bottle contains a little of this sediment. Old wine bottles with corks make excellent storage containers, as will any glass bottle that has a screw-top lid. Make sure you store these in a dark cupboard away from direct sunlight.

BICARBONATE OF SODA

Because bicarbonate of soda (or baking soda) is a natural substance, it can be used quite safely without doing any harm to the environment, which is great for us grannies who are not quite sure what 'going green' means. I always thought it meant you looked a little sickly if someone said you were turning green! Quite simply, bicarbonate of soda is sodium bicarbonate, a substance which is found naturally in mineral deposits around the world. The wonders of bicarbonate of soda were first discovered by bakers when they found that it had the capability of trapping air bubbles in the ingredients of bread or cakes, causing them to rise. Then it was discovered to work well as an antacid for upset stomachs, a truly fantastic odour absorber, and, in later years, as a household cleaner. It is used in the manufacture of glass, paper, soaps, and in many of our household detergents, and does a great job of softening hard water, too. Manufacturers have realized its potential for a long time and certain toothpastes now contain bicarbonate of soda to help whiten your teeth.

Having sung the praises of bicarbonate of soda here is a list of things that this natural powder can help you with.

acid indigestion, cold sores, cystitis, deodorant, dry skin, gargling, gum massage, heartburn, insect bites and stings, mouthwash, nappy rash, removing odours, skin irritations, splinters, stomach ache, sunburn, whitening teeth, and warts.

I remember a time in Devon when I was recovering from childhood measles. My skin was still quite itchy and red and granny said she had just the answer. She filled for me a tub of lovely warm water and then tipped something in, the smell of which reminded me of the apple scones she used to bake for our tea.

Granny's Bathtime Treat

You will need
90 g (3½ oz) bicarbonate of soda
250 g (9 oz) sea salt
2 to 3 teaspoons ground cinnamon
A few drops of apple essential oil
A few drops vanilla extract or oil

Method
1. Mix the salt and bicarbonate of soda in a large bowl.
2. Add the oils to the bowl and stir well to coat the mixture. Then add the cinnamon, mix well, cover the bowl and leave for about an hour so the powder absorbs the scents.
3. Store in a glass jar with a lid and use about a handful when you want a special treat at bathtime.

GINGER (*Zingiber officinale*)
We all know about the benefits of ginger as a flavouring agent, but are you aware that it has been used medicinally since ancient times? It is an underground stem or rhizome, which is either sold in this fleshy form, as a dried spice, or in a crystallized form. In China, ginger has been used for over 2,000 years and is considered to be a healing gift from God. It was commonly used to cleanse and warm the body, and in the treatment of diarrhoea and nausea, and medical practitioners around the world are now aware of its many benefits. It is an antioxidant, anti-inflammatory, carminative (reduces flatulence), anticoagulant, can reduce blood pressure and cholesterol levels, and is also a vasodilator. Because of its antimicrobial properties it can also be used to treat minor sores and wounds. In the West Indies ginger is used for the treatment of urinary tract infections, while herbal practitioners in Nigeria use it to treat malaria and yellow fever.

Ginger can be used in various forms to treat any of the following:

arthritis, bad breath, bowel disorders, circulatory problems, colds and flu, colon cleansing, cramps, digestion problems, fatigue, headaches, hives, hot flushes, inflammation, motion sickness, morning sickness, muscle aches, nausea and vomiting, pain, respiratory disorders, and sores and wounds.

Because ginger can cause upset stomachs if taken in large quantities and also act as a menstrual stimulant, you should always be cautious and only take small amounts at any one time. Ginger should also not be given to children under two years of age.

As explained earlier, my sister and I were not good travellers and my mother always kept a jar of crystallized ginger for our journeys down to Devon. Here is the recipe she used and one I have continued to use for my own children who were also notoriously bad at stomaching long car journeys.

Granny's Ginger Saviour

You will need
500 g (1 lb) thinly sliced peeled fresh ginger
granulated sugar
water
extra granulated sugar for coating

Method
1. Place the prepared ginger in a heavy saucepan and cover with water.
2. Cook gently until the ginger is tender, about 30 minutes.
3. Drain off the water.
4. Weigh the cooked ginger and measure an equal amount of sugar.
5. Return the ginger to the saucepan, add the sugar and 3 tablespoons of water.
6. Bring to the boil, stirring frequently, and cook until the ginger becomes transparent and the liquid has almost evaporated.
7. Reduce heat and cook, stirring constantly, until almost dry.
8. Toss cooled ginger in sugar to coat.
9. Store crystallized (candied) ginger in an airtight jar for up to three months.

LEMONS

For me the sight and smell of a lemon takes me back to sitting in granny's garden with an enormous jug of her homemade lemonade. None of that nasty fizzy stuff they try to sell in supermarkets, just a wonderful cloudy drink that was so refreshing you just wanted to come back for more. Everyone knows of their value in cooking, but perhaps it is time to take a closer look at this bright yellow little fruit for there is far more you can do with it than just make lemonade or squeeze it on your fish and chips.

In traditional medicine the lemon has been widely recognized for its healing powers and it has been used in many different ways for centuries. In fact, the Romans believed that it was so powerful that it would act as an antidote to any type of poison.

Lemons have so many beneficial properties that, taken regularly in water they can help to strengthen your immune system. For example, if you have a cold or flu, drink some lemon juice diluted in water and it will not only relieve the symptoms it will also halt the progress of the infection. Why? Because it has both antibacterial and antiviral properties.

Lemon juice is also very effective in dealing with digestive problems, including sickness, nausea, and heartburn and, taken in warm water, it can relieve the symptoms of sore throats and tonsillitis. Because lemon is also a diuretic, it is great for people with urinary tract infections and can also be beneficial in treating arthritis and rheumatism because it helps to flush out all the bad toxins.

When applied externally, lemon juice can help treat many infections and hasten the healing of minor wounds.

Now you are aware of just some of the benefits of taking lemon juice, I want to list all the nutrients found in this little fruit so that you can get an idea of just how valuable it is in our daily lives.

Calcium

Our bodies need calcium to maintain the health of our bones and teeth, particularly in our twilight years, as a long-term calcium deficiency could lead to osteoporosis or crumbly bones. After the age of around 50 both men and women begin to lose calcium from their bones, which leaves us more prone to fractures. Walking helps to maintain strong bones and is the best exercise for preventing osteoporosis, but start your day with a glass of water containing a teaspoon of lemon juice and you are boosting your calcium intake as well.

Citric acid

Citric acid is found naturally in all citrus fruits, and lemons and limes have high concentrations, accounting for their bitter taste. Citric acid has many benefits to the human body and in particular, the digestive system. It can help to break down fats and therefore assist in regulating the body's natural pH levels. Citric acid can also help prevent diarrhoea and urinary tract infections. For those people who suffer from kidney stones, the presence of citric acid in the body will inhibit the stones from forming and can also break up any small stones that are already present in the body.

Flavonoids

Flavonoids are nutrients found in fruit and vegetables that are beneficial to the human body. It is believed that flavonoids can protect against damage in blood vessels, therefore decreasing the risk of cardiovascular diseases. Recent research has also shown that they can play a part in cancer prevention and help build up the body's entire immune system. The flavonoid found in lemons is called hesperitin, which has been found to have an anti-inflammatory effect. Tests have shown that hesperitin can help to reduce cholesterol and high blood pressure.

Limonoids

Limonoids are abundant in citrus fruit and account for the scent of fresh lemon peel. Limonoids are currently being used in cancer research and, unlike many of the conventional cancer treatments, have not shown any side effects. It is too soon to say exactly how successful this natural plant chemical will be, but it has shown other therapeutic effects such as being antiviral, antifungal, and antibacterial.

Magnesium

Magnesium is found naturally in both plants and animals and is a mineral that serves a vital role within the human body. Our bones store magnesium which, in turn, helps in the production of the hormone calcitonin. This is used to produce vital calcium in our bones and to control the level of acidity in our blood. Magnesium also helps to keep our hearts beating regularly. Insufficient magnesium can lead to muscle cramps, high blood pressure, fatigue, and migraines.

Pectins

Pectin is found in the rind and peel of citrus fruits and is probably best known as the agent used for making jam set. It also has some other extraordinary benefits to the human body in that it can help to dispel toxins and also promotes cardiovascular health and normal cell growth. It has many pharmaceutical uses as well, one of which is as a carrier for a variety of drugs that need to be released slowly into the system.

Phosphorus

Phosphorus is a vital part of health and life and is a mineral that can be found in all living cells. It is essential to the structure and function of much of the human body, particularly in the forming of bones and teeth, as it assists in the absorption and use of calcium, magnesium, and vitamin C. It also plays an important role in keeping the body's muscular system working efficiently, maintaining the regular beat of our hearts. Phosphorus also helps in the transformation of nutrients into energy and plays a vital role in the digestive system, nervous system, and regulating the body's natural pH levels. Lemons contain a small proportion of phosphorus, but you can find higher amounts in nuts, seeds, cereal grains, meat, poultry, and fish, so eating a healthy diet is the best way to ensure your body gets a sufficient supply.

Vitamin C

Vitamin C is the most common vitamin required for good health and lemons are full of it. This vitamin plays a vital role in the correct functioning of the most vital organs in your body, so you can see how important it is that you get a good supply on a regular basis. As your body is unable to store vitamin C, you need to replenish it daily otherwise there is a risk that you will suffer from a deficiency. By maintaining a diet that is rich in vitamin C, it will not only keep you healthy but it will improve the look of your skin as well. The greatest sources of vitamin C are of course the citrus fruits and their juices, but many other fruit and vegetables are rich in it as well – red peppers, parsley, broccoli, cauliflower, strawberries, papaya, kiwi, cantaloupe melon, cabbage, tomatoes, raspberries, celery, spinach, pineapple, watermelon, cranberries, and guava.

Vitamin C is particularly important to those of you who still like to have the odd puff on a cigarette. The reason for this is because the body of a smoker uses up more of this vitamin than that of a non-smoker. It is also worth pointing out that taking anything in excess can be harmful to your health, so do not overdose on vitamin C believing you are doing your body a favour.

Having given you all the mind-boggling facts about lemons and their advantages to our health you are probably ready to take a break. Take a little time to make my lovely old-fashioned lemonade and then sit down with a refreshing glass and see how quickly it will revive you. You can make it as sweet as you like by adding sugar or honey and you can rest easy that it is free from any artificial colours or flavours which might send your grandchildren into a state of hyperactive frenzy!

Granny's Lemonade Refresher

You will need   *Serves 8*
10 large unwaxed lemons
115 g (4 oz) caster sugar (or to taste)
1.5 litres (2¼ pints) water
Sprigs of mint for decoration

Method
1. Pare the rind from nine of the lemons using a vegetable peeler so that it is nice and thin, taking care to avoid any white pith. Squeeze out and strain the juice from the lemons to make up 450 ml (15 fl oz).
2. Put the lemon rind into a large, heatproof bowl. Add the sugar and pour in 1.5 litres (2¼ pints) of boiling water. Keep stirring until the sugar has completely dissolved. Cover the bowl and leave to stand for 30 minutes.
3. Strain the liquid into a large jug and then stir in the lemon juice. Cover and refrigerate for about two hours, or until it is well chilled. Serve with sprigs of mint and ice cubes.

This lemonade will keep for about a week in a refrigerator.

HERBS

The amazing power of herbs has been harnessed for thousands of years and there have been volumes written on their health properties. As well as providing numerous remedies, herbs also contain vitamins, minerals and antioxidants like all fruit and vegetables. Herbal remedies are gentle, easy to use, and very effective for numerous ailments. It is hard to equal the value of a plant freshly picked from your own garden or from the hedgerow as you take your daily constitutional. However, before using any herb make sure you know exactly what you have picked, because it is easy to confuse certain herbs with a poisonous variety which would not be beneficial to your health. I bought myself a book many years ago to assist me; it was called *I Spy of Herbs*. I doubt this is still in print, but there must be other useful sources out there. I am not going to use anything in this book that is obscure and difficult to get hold of, just everyday herbs that you can grow in your garden or common wild plants such as nettle or wild rose.

Herbs are rich in antioxidants, which help to combat everyday pollutants such as the fumes from car exhausts and smoke. Eating foods rich in antioxidants reduces the damage to our body cells and consequently helps to keep us looking healthier and younger. Echinacea (or Cone Flower) is a fine example of this as it can boost our immune system and helps us fight off cold and flu viruses.

St John's Wort is another beneficial plant as it works as an antidepressant but has fewer side effects than any prescribed drug. Chamomile is a herb that can quickly soothe an upset stomach or aid in a good night's sleep. Thyme has mild antiseptic properties and can help ease sore throats and coughs.

Sage can help to calm the nerves, improve digestion, and help ease congestion from mucus if you are suffering from a bad cough and cold. Rosemary is excellent for improving circulation, stimulates the liver into eliminating toxins from the body, eases joint and head pain, and relieves cold symptoms. Mint is great for aiding digestive problems, relaxes the mind, and can help with headaches. Marigold is an excellent healing herb and can ease cuts, burns, and bruises. Whether you want a natural solution to a headache or a stomach ache, or simply want to boost your immune system, there is always a herb that can do the job for you. For example, parsley is one of the most important herbs for providing vitamins to the body and contains more vitamin C than any vegetable or fruit. It also contains twice as much iron as spinach and is a good source of manganese, calcium, and potassium. It also contains flavonoids that act as antioxidants and is rich in vitamin A.

The list of herbs is endless and I won't look at them all in this chapter. What I would like to do is go into more detail about how to store your herbs so that they are always ready to use even if you are unable to pick them fresh. Of course you can always grow a few of the more common ones in pots on your windowsill, but by drying some as well you can keep your larder well stocked.

Drying your herbs
The key to drying herbs is to do it as quickly as possible so that none of the nutrients are lost during the drying process, and so they retain their natural colour and smell. If you use a microwave or an oven to dry your herbs then much of the oil content and flavour will be lost, so drying naturally in the air is the only answer. Make sure you pick your herbs before they have had a chance to flower and pick them in the morning before the midday sun has started to make them wilt.

Shake the herbs to get rid of any insects and make sure there is no moisture left on the leaves as this will cause them to go mouldy. Lay them out on a sheet of greaseproof paper in an airy room, preferably one that has a through draught. If you want to use the stems as well, as in sage or peppermint, it is best to make up small bunches and hang them from the ceiling. A rubber band is ideal for this, but check periodically that the bundle is not starting to slip as the stems will shrink as they start to dry. If you want to collect the seeds of herbs such as fennel or caraway, then simply place the seed heads on a tray in a well-aired room and leave them until the seeds fall off.

Storing dried herbs

Store your dried herbs or seeds in airtight containers such as jam jars with tight-fitting lids or resealable freezer bags. Make sure you label and date all your containers so that they do not get mixed up later on. Your herbs will retain their flavour and scent for longer if you store them whole and crush them when you are ready to use them. If you see any signs of mould make sure you throw the affected leaves away, otherwise they will contaminate the entire batch. Keep the containers in a cool, dry place away from direct sunlight. Dried herbs are best used up within a year; as soon as you see that they are starting to lose their colour, they are also losing the beneficial nutrients required.

WORD OF CAUTION

The recommended dosage is one teaspoon of dried herbs to a tablespoon of water, but be cautious when treating small children; always consult a doctor first. Do not allow any illness to continue for more than a couple of days before seeking medical advice.

Another point to bear in mind is that until your body gets used to a certain herb, you or your patient could experience side effects. These side effects are less common than from using proprietary drugs and usually not so severe, but if, for example, you experience an upset stomach after taking a herbal tea, it might be your body's way of saying it is learning how to process it. Give it a few more tries, but if the side effects continue then stop taking it immediately.

ALOE VERA (*Aloe barbadensis*)

Although the aloe vera plant resembles a cactus, it is in fact part of the lily family. Its use for medicinal purposes can be traced back over 6,000 years to Egypt, where it was known as the 'plant of immortality'. Aloe vera was presented as a burial gift to pharaohs who had passed into the next world.

Its first recorded use in medicine was as a laxative as far back as 2200 BC, which has been proved by writing on old Sumerian clay tablets singing the plant's praises. The fleshy leaf of the aloe vera plant is structured in layers. It has a thick outer layer that protects the leaf from external damage and helps in fluid retention during dry spells. The next layer is the sap, which is really bitter and helps protect the plant from predators. The inner layer is the mucilage gel, from which most of the benefits of the plant are extracted.

The aloe vera plant reaches maturity at around two to three years of age, and this is when it contains its greatest nutritional properties. The gel, once extracted from the plant, should not be left in the air for more than two hours as it oxidizes rapidly, which will cause it to lose its therapeutic properties. Keeping it in a container in the refrigerator will neutralize the undesirable effects of oxygenation. The gel is invaluable for its anti-inflammatory, antibacterial, and antifungal properties, and can be used for any number of healing processes. It can be dabbed on, eaten, drunk, or chewed, depending on the level of treatment required.

The wonders of aloe vera

- Traditionally taken orally as a laxative.
- Used externally to heal wounds and for various skin conditions.
- Women all over the world use the gel on their skin to keep it supple and free from blemishes.
- Used externally for burns and sunburn.
- Taken orally for diabetes, asthma, epilepsy, and osteoarthritis.
- In ayurvedic medicine, aloe vera gel is a tonic for the female reproductive system.
- It is claimed to prevent hair loss when rubbed into the scalp.
- It helps fight viruses if used in a high concentration and applied directly to the virus.
- Aloe vera also has a hormone that helps accelerate the growth of new cells.
- Can help relieve itching and swelling of irritated skin.

Today, aloe vera can be found in hundreds of different skin products and it has also been approved as a natural food flavouring. The part that is traditionally used as a laxative is a substance called 'latex' which is the sap or juice that surrounds the gel. It is extremely bitter and, a word of warning, this substance is very potent when taken by mouth.

The beauty of the aloe vera plant is that it can be grown very easily indoors – no green fingers required here! You can buy them from any garden centre or, alternatively, take a cutting from a friend's plant and propagate it yourself. It is an attractive plant to have around the house and will always be there should you need to get some gel quickly to put on a burn or a graze. My granny was never without a plant or two and my kitchen windowsill is always full of little cuttings so that I have got a constant supply.

Side effects of aloe vera are usually minimal compared with many other medicines on the market. Aloe vera is a herbal, natural method and when used properly should not cause any side effects.

THE HEALING POWER OF VEGETABLES

From a small child I was always told to eat up my vegetables because they are good for you. However, like many youngsters, I preferred to eat a raw carrot rather than a cooked one, and a Brussels sprout was usually surreptitiously dropped on the floor in the hope that the dog would eat it – needless to say it never did! I used to think it was a ploy on the part of mother to get me to eat vegetables; little did I know then that what she was telling me was actually the truth. Raw vegetables, in particular, contain many nutrients and plenty of fibre which help to keep our bodies in good shape. Never overcook vegetables as they will lose a lot of their natural goodness, but lightly steamed ones are nearly as good as raw. Alternatively you can put them through a juicer and use as a healthy drink. Below is a list of just a few of the vegetables and how they help our systems to work efficiently.

Asparagus – is rich in asparagine which is an amino acid and acts as a mild diuretic.

Beetroot – is high in vitamins and minerals which are excellent for strengthening the gall bladder and for regenerating blood.

Broccoli and **Brussels sprouts** – are rich in vitamins and minerals and also provide protein.

Cabbage and **kale** – provide a rich source of vitamins and minerals as well as sulphur compounds.

Carrots – these little wonders contain a very complete nutrition to provide our bodies with the essential enzymes, vitamins, and minerals. They are also an excellent source of beta-carotene, which the body converts to vitamin A, and an antioxidant like vitamins E and C.

Celery – is nature's best toothbrush. By chewing celery it helps to stimulate the flow of saliva, helps fight cavities, and also neutralizes plaque acids that attack teeth. Celery is also high in minerals and a significant source of magnesium.

Cucumber – is high in potassium.

Collards – these are members of the cabbage family that produce dark green leaves but no heads. They are rich in calcium, iron, and vitamin A.

Fennel – this has its own distinctive flavour and is one of the ingredients in liquorice. It has all the same nutritional values as celery, is an effective treatment for respiratory congestion, and is a common ingredient in many cough remedies.

Onions – these contain a number of sulphides similar to those found in garlic, which help in lowering blood lipids and blood pressure. They are also a rich source of fructo-oligosaccharides which help to suppress the growth of potentially harmful bacteria.

Peppers – both sweet and hot, are packed with vitamins and carotenoids which is a vitamin A-type compound.

Potatoes – are a very good source of vitamin C, vitamin B6, copper, potassium, manganese, and dietary fibre.

Radishes – the radish and its leaves are an excellent source of vitamin C, folic acid, calcium, and potassium.

Spinach – a dark green leaf that is very rich in iron and other vitamins and minerals.

Sweet potatoes – are another good source of beta-carotene.

Even though consumption of both fruit and vegetables has gone up in recent years, apparently there are still families that do not eat them every day. Try to make sure your family – and of course yourself – eat the recommended 'five a day' in some form or another. My grandchildren have been raised on vegetables and fruit and believe it or not the first thing they eat off their plates is anything green!

HOW DO I KNOW?

I have already stressed the importance of eating foods that are rich in antioxidants and one way to judge just how much is in a particular fruit or vegetable is by its colour. The brighter the colour, the more useful vitamins you will obtain from eating it. When it comes to antioxidants, berries are definitely the leaders – blackberries, raspberries, strawberries, cranberries, and blueberries are all high in flavonoids which have similar effects to antioxidants.

Green tea is another good source of flavonoids, so try and replace your regular morning tea with a green variety. Amazingly, coffee is also another good source of antioxidants, but it should be taken black to reap the full benefit. Dark chocolate is also rich in antioxidants, so you see, sometimes the foods we love can actually benefit our health.

The easy way to make sure that you have enough natural antioxidants in your diet is to eat fruit as a snack rather than your favourite biscuit or cake. I am not saying cut these out totally; allow yourself a treat at least once a week. When I visit my daughter each Wednesday, we always allow ourselves a treat of a cream tea or a slice of cake and then eat healthily the rest of the week. Dry fruits are also good natural sources of antioxidants, so include dates, prunes, and raisins in your snacks as well. Spices are also beneficial so not only will they give your food flavour, they will supply you with vitamins and work on keeping you young at the same time.

WHOLE GRAINS

Having explained about the antioxidant properties of fruit and vegetables, now is the time to move on to whole grains and their benefits. Whole grains are an even better source of phytochemicals and antioxidants than fruit and vegetables. They are an excellent source of all the B vitamins, vitamin E, magnesium, iron, and fibre, as well as other valuable antioxidants not found in fruit and vegetables. The common types of whole grains we use today are – wild rice, brown rice, whole wheat, oatmeal, whole oats, barley, whole rye, bulgar wheat, and popcorn.

Whole grains have been shown to reduce the risk of heart disease by decreasing cholesterol levels, and reducing blood pressure and blood clotting. An easy way to increase your intake of whole grains is to:

• Have a slice of wholegrain bread instead of your normal white.
• Have a serving of wholegrain breakfast cereal each morning.
• When baking your favourite biscuits, cakes or pancakes, substitute half the white flour with wholewheat flour.
• If you are making soup, add some brown rice, wild rice or barley.
• Snack on unsweetened popcorn instead of sweeties.

When determining if a packaged food contains whole grain in its list of ingredients, do not be fooled by the colour of the food. Brown, does not necessarily mean that it contains wholegrain products. Look for the word 'whole' or look for the 'wholegrain stamp'. If it says it is a 'good source' then the product will contain at least half a serving of whole grains, an 'excellent' source contains at least one serving, so use this as your guide.

PULSES

Pulses are all members of the legume family and include chickpeas, peas, lentils, beans, and lupins. Pulses are a beneficial addition to any diet as they are low in fat, high in fibre, have a low glycaemic index, are high in protein and nutrients, and help to lower cholesterol. It is easy to keep some pulses in your larder or freezer and they also have a long shelf life. Baked beans are a great way of introducing children to pulses, but be careful that they do not contain a lot of extra sugar and salt so read the label first.

Dried pulses should be stored in airtight containers and if they are kept in the dark the seeds will keep their colour much longer. Remember, though, you will need to allow time for soaking dried pulses, so you might like to consider leaving them overnight when planning the next day's dinner.

Here are some easy ways to make sure you have a good supply of pulses in your diet:

• Have some baked beans on toast for breakfast or as a quick snack. You can always sprinkle some grated cheese on top if you want to make it an extra special treat.
• Use hummus in your sandwiches instead of margarine or butter, or use it as a dip with some raw vegetables.
• Add some pulses to soups, stews, casseroles, curries, or even salads.
• Add some pulses to your stir fries; sugar snap peas make a wonderful addition.

If you would rather prepare your own pulses than buying canned or dried, then cook a large batch at a time as cooked pulses freeze exceptionally well. Divide them into portions and put into freezer bags so you only take out what you need. If, like me, you are old school and still like to use a pressure cooker, it can reduce the cooking time by half and minimize the loss of nutrients at the same time.

You have taken a trip through granny's larder and discovered many of the healthy ingredients she always kept to hand. We all love to eat and to many people it is one of the most important aspects of their lives. The type of food we eat says a lot about who we are and provides us with the essential energy and nutrition to live a healthy life. You will probably read many conflicting reports about what is good for you and what is bad, but the general rule of thumb is that if you eat a varied diet with plenty of fruit and vegetables you can't go far wrong. In my granny's day food was not so easy to come by and it was down to the individual to grow their own where possible. By doing that, at least the individual was certain that the food had not been genetically modified or coloured with some artificial chemical to make it more appealing.

Granny's Breakfast Muesli

You will need   *Serves 8*
375 g (13 oz) porridge oats
50 g (2 oz) wheatgerm
30 g (1 oz) wheat bran
50 g (2 oz) oat bran
150 g (5 oz) sultanas
50 g (2 oz) dried berries, such as blueberries or cranberries
30 g (1 oz) chopped nuts (of choice)

Method
Mix all the ingredients in a large bowl. Serve with milk, soya milk, yogurt, or fresh fruit. To sweeten add a little brown sugar, honey, or maple syrup.
You can store the muesli in an airtight container for up to two months.

HONEY

My grandparents had two beehives at the end of the allotment and I remember as a young girl, being fascinated when grandad put on a pair of white overalls, covered his head with something that resembled a space helmet and donned a pair of old leather gloves. He made me stand at a distance when he opened the hives, but seeing all the bees busy making their honeycomb used to give me a thrill. I was never stung during those sessions, but I do remember grandad jumping occasionally if a stray bee gave him a warning sting – needless to say granny always had a quick cure up her sleeve. Granny used to bottle the honey – wax as well – and my sister and I loved to spread it on our toast or granny's scrummy crumpets for our tea.

Of course the benefits of honey go far beyond just its taste. It is a natural source of sugar which can provide our bodies with energy and strength which means you don't get tired so quickly. If you are feeling a little lethargic in the morning, honey spread on some warm toast will give you the surge of energy you require. No need for those newfangled so-called energy drinks, when there is a jar of honey in the larder. Honey has also been known for its healing properties for thousands of years as it contains a number of antibacterial properties. These properties inhibit the growth of certain bacteria and can help to keep external wounds clean and free from infection. It is great for treating wounds, burns, and cuts as it is able to absorb moisture from the air and therefore promote faster healing.

Honey also works well in building up an immunity as it is an antioxidant which can keep you healthy and help you to fight off disease. If you start every day with a cup of warm water that contains a spoonful of honey and some lemon juice, then this will act as a cleansing tonic to help your system stave off germs.

With the advancement in medical science during the 20th century, honey has taken more of a back seat; that was until the discovery of a specific type of honey called Manuka.

Manuka honey

Manuka honey is produced by bees that gather nectar from flowers on the shrub *Leptospermum scoparium* (or manuka bush) which grows wild on the north and south islands of New Zealand. Manuka honey contains very powerful antibacterial, antimicrobial, antiviral, antioxidant, antiseptic, anti-inflammatory, and antifungal properties, making it extremely effective in the treatment of a wide variety of health conditions:

aches and pains, acid reflux disease, acne, arthritis, athlete's foot, blisters, burns, chronic wounds, cold sores, eczema and dermatitis, gum disease, infections, insect bites, MRSA/ staphylococcus infections, nail fungus, pressure sores, psoriasis, rashes, ringworm, skin ulcers, sore throat, stomach ulcers, surgical wounds, wounds and abrasions, and wrinkles.

Granny's Honey Hangover Cure

Honey is really gentle on the stomach and can quickly cure a hangover because it contains natural sugars such as fructose which are known to speed up the oxidation of alcohol by the liver. This acts as a sobering agent, so why not try this remedy when you are suffering the effects of a heavy night out.

You will need
15 ml (1 tbsp) liquid honey
80 ml (5 tbsp) orange juice
70 ml (4 tbsp) natural yogurt

Method
Blend them all together and enjoy the beneficial effects.

Chapter Three

General Health

Natural Remedies for General Health

Granny shuffles to the bathroom
Teeth missing and ankles slim
She mumbles something silly
About wanting to join a gym!

If you chuckle at the thought of granny trying to keep upright on a treadmill with her stockings round her ankles, then more fool you. Many people, once they reach retirement age, are joining gyms in an effort to stave off the advancing years. Actually they are probably the ones who will have the last laugh because they don't pay nearly as much in annual fees as the youngsters, and many are entitled to free sessions if it is recommended by their doctors. Keeping fit by doing moderate exercise is probably the best way to maintain a reasonable level of health and, combined with a healthy diet, granny is probably in much better shape than some of you who have a tendency to become couch potatoes.

Home remedies and natural cures for minor ailments, using everyday things found around the house and garden, are becoming more and more popular. They are inexpensive, contain no harmful chemicals, very rarely give any side effects, and take some pressure off doctors who can then concentrate on more serious ailments.

You cannot put a price on your health or that of your loved ones, so if you can contribute to keeping them in tip-top shape your efforts will be well rewarded. Many people are going back to using old traditional remedies in preference to proprietary drugs. Although we all know that antibiotics are invaluable in treating certain illnesses, if prescribed too often they can kill off many of the good bacteria in our bodies, which can mean it takes us longer to recover. Add to that the plethora of unpleasant side effects such as nausea, diarrhoea, and drowsiness, and it is no wonder we look for more natural ways to combat some of the minor everyday ailments.

The kitchen is a great place to start as scientists are discovering more and more positive properties in our everyday foods. So whether we want to boost our immune system, treat a child's acne, or just soothe a nasty sore thoat, why not turn to some of granny's old remedies which aren't nearly as archaic as they might sound.

Remember, if the symptoms continue after treatment, or the patient seems in a lot of discomfort, it is always advisable to seek professional medical advice.

Granny's Cure-alls

ACNE

Acne is usually associated with teenagers and can be very distressing, leaving them quite withdrawn. It is an inflammatory condition of the sweat glands and hair follicles which results in spots or small cysts forming on the skin of the face, neck, chest, and shoulders. There are several types of acne, the most common being blackheads, which can be a major embarrassment at an age when people tend to be oversensitive about their personal appearance. Acne can very often be triggered by bad eating habits, particularly excessively fatty foods or those with a high sugar content. Chronic constipation is another cause of acne, because the body is trying to rid itself of excess toxins.

Treatment

- Firstly make sure the person concerned changes his or her eating habits. Their diet should include plenty of fibre, fruit, and vegetables and they should avoid any fried foods or those with excessive amounts of sugar. Encourage the person to drink plenty of water with a little lemon juice added to flush out the toxins.

- Grind some orange peel with water in a pestle and mortar and apply to affected areas.

- Apply lemon juice regularly to reduce pimples and acne.

- As long as you don't mind the smell, rubbing garlic on the affected areas several times a day has been known to cure even the worst bouts of acne. If you want to purify the bloodstream of any toxins, eat three cloves of raw garlic daily for a month. This might sound a bit drastic, but it really works.

- Grate some cucumber and apply it to the affected areas for 15 to 20 minutes each day. If used regularly it can prevent the recurrence of spots and blackheads.

ANAEMIA

I used to soak some dates in honey and eat them regularly for breakfast to keep anaemia at bay and it seems to have worked for me. Anaemia is one of the most common ailments affecting humans. It is a condition in which the number of red blood cells decreases. These cells are vital for good health as they carry oxygen to the tissues; if they drop too low then the person can experience weakness, fatigue, lack of energy, and bouts of dizziness. The skin usually looks pale and the patient will often complain of headaches and tiredness. Anaemia can often follow after a heavy loss of blood, particularly during times of menstruation. Diet is very important, especially during pregnancy, so read up on foods that are rich in iron and zinc and also those that contain vitamin C. Taking walks in sunlight can also help to stimulate the body's production of red blood cells.

Treatment

- Vitamin B12 is essential for curing anaemia and can be found in red meats such as liver and kidneys.

- Honey is one of the best things to take for building up haemo-globin in the body. This is because it contains iron, copper, and manganese.

- Spinach is a valuable source of iron which helps in the formation of red blood cells.

- Beetroot is very beneficial in treating anaemia as it has a high iron content and many other necessary minerals and vitamins that help in the formation of red blood cells. It can either be eaten as a vegetable or used in a drink with other vegetables.

- Soya milk, which is easy to digest, is another source of iron and protein and can be used as you would cow's milk.

- Avoid foods that rid the body of essential iron. These foods include white bread, white rice, and sugar. The emphasis should be on eating raw vegetables, fresh fruit, seeds, nuts, and grains, all of which will replenish the body with iron.

ATHLETE'S FOOT

Athlete's foot is a fungal infection that thrives on dead skin cells. It occurs mainly between the toes where it can cause itching and often a burning sensation as well. In bad cases you may notice blisters and inflammation, which can often ooze and become really unpleasant. This type of fungus loves warm and damp conditions, so a foot that has been shut up all day in a shoe, is prone to athlete's foot. This is particularly true of runners or other athletes – hence the name – as their feet tend to sweat and the socks and liners of the shoes can become quite moist.

Always make sure you wash your hands carefully after treating athlete's foot as it is very infectious and you can easily spread it to your other foot or to another person.

Treatment

- Tea tree oil has antifungal properties, so treat the affected area.

- Prepare a solution of one part white vinegar to four parts of water. Soak your feet for at least 30 minutes twice a day.

- Baking soda also has antifungal properties, so sprinkle some powder between your toes and then rinse off after about 15 minutes.

- Try to avoid eating anything that contains a lot of yeast. Avoid alcohol, sugary foods, fizzy drinks, and too many grains. Make sure you eat plenty of fresh fruit and vegetables and include raw garlic in your diet.

- Make sure you dry your feet thoroughly after taking a bath, shower, or going swimming. Only wear cotton socks and make sure your gym shoes are cleaned regularly.

BACKACHE

Backache is one of the most common complaints and affects between 80 and 90 per cent of adult men and women. Much of this is caused by modern sedentary lifestyles, hazardous work conditions or stress, which can lead to muscle spasms in the back. This is

not surprising considering the back has to bear the weight of the entire body. Poor posture can also play a part in backache, along with sitting for too long in one position without moving, and more serious illnesses connected with the kidneys or prostate, so it is probably advisable to seek medical advice before starting any form of treatment.

Treatment

● Good old garlic is used again in the treatment of backache. Warmed garlic oil (*see page 30*) rubbed into the sore part of the back two to three times a day, for about 15 days, should help ease the pain.

● Red pepper contains a marvellous pain-relieving chemical called capsaicin which is so potent it is used as an ingredient in many proprietary analgesics. Mash the pepper and add it to any non-perfumed skin cream, then rub into the affected area.

● A mixture of menthol and camphor can also help relieve back pain. Menthol is a natural ingredient found in the mint family and camphor occurs in spike lavender, hyssop, and coriander. Grind the leaves of both menthol and camphor plants to a paste, add a little olive oil, and massage well into the affected area.

● For a really ancient home remedy, apply raw potato in the form of a poultice. This treatment is particularly good for pain in the lower part of the back or lumbar region.

● Anyone suffering from back pain should avoid fatty, spicy, fried foods or any that are packed with sugar. Only drink tea and coffee occasionally and make sure you eat plenty of raw vegetables such as tomatoes, carrots, cabbage, cucumber, radish, and lettuce and at least two portions of lightly steamed vegetables each day.

BAD BREATH

Bad breath or halitosis is another common condition. The most common cause is dental decay or diseased gums, so regular trips to the dentist are essential. (I hated the dentist as a child, but modern dentistry is so advanced the experience is not nearly so bad these days.) Even the tiniest little hole in a tooth can provide a place for germs to live and breed, which often results in a foul odour. Upset stomachs and constipation can also lead to bad breath, as can conditions of the nose, throat, or respiratory tract, in particular sinusitis which can cause a discharge at the back of the throat.

Treatment

- Of all the home treatments, fenugreek has proved to be the most successful. Fenugreek seeds are one of the world's oldest medicinal herbs and can be bought whole or dried as a dull yellow powder made from the roasted seeds. If you like growing your own herbs, it is a hardy little plant that likes full sun and a well-drained soil. The seedpods should be harvested and dried in mid-autumn and the seeds stored in an airtight container in a dry, dark place. To treat bad breath with fenugreek, make a tea from the seeds by putting one teaspoon of seeds in half a litre of boiling water. Allow the tea to infuse for 15 minutes and then strain and drink as normal tea.

- If bad breath is due to a stomach disorder, then avocado is effective in removing any decomposing matter from the intestines.

- Make sure the patient drinks plenty of water to wash out any toxins, as a dry mouth can lead to bad breath.

- Unripe guava is another useful remedy for halitosis. It is rich in tannic, malic, oxalic, and phosphoric acids as well as being rich in calcium, oxalate, and manganese. Chewing guava is exellent for your teeth and gums and by promoting healthy teeth you should improve your bad breath as well. You can also chew the tender leaves of the guava tree to stop bad breath, but you may find these difficult to get hold of.

● Parsley is a really good cure for bad breath as it has large amounts of chlorophyll. Boil two teacups of water and add several sprigs of coarsely chopped parsley. If you like you can also add three whole cloves to spice it up a little and leave the mixture to infuse. Stir occasionally while the mixture is cooling, then strain and use as a mouthwash or gargle several times a day. Alternatively, you can munch on a piece of parsley after meals to help sweeten the breath.

● Boil a few anise seeds with a cupful of water for a few minutes. Strain and you will have a pleasant liquorice-flavoured drink or mouthwash.

● Peppermint is also well known for sweetening the breath, so make a tea infusion by pouring boiling water over mint leaves. This drink is also good for the digestion.

● Make sure you clean your teeth regularly, using floss to remove any particles that might be trapped.

BALDNESS

The men in my family seem to have a good head of hair, especially my father who had a mass of pure white hair even in his nineties. Unfortunately, not all men are so lucky and would do anything to stop their receding hairline. Women don't seem to suffer to the same extent, so perhaps that is why we are not as patient as we should be when dealing with someone who is losing their hair. Baldness is very often genetic, but sometimes it can be the result of severe stress. Many men choose to shave their hair off, which luckily is trendy today, but not so in my grandad's time.

To stop premature balding you need a substance that will stop the conversion of the male hormone, testosterone, into dihydro-testosterone (or DHT). It is believed that it is DHT that kills off the hair follicles. The following are thought to help stop the formation of DHT to a slight degree, so you might like to have a go, but I can't promise you will have a thick head of hair overnight!

Treatment

- To deal with premature hair loss, it is important to follow a well-balanced diet, paying special attention to all the necessary nutrients required to slow down the loss of hair. Vegetables should be high on the list, with spinach, celery leaves, and cauliflower eaten on a regular basis. Concentrate on foods that contain omega 3 and omega 3 fatty acids – fish, soya, nuts, and sunflower seeds as examples – as these foods nourish the scalp.

- Drinking one cup of lettuce and spinach juice daily can prevent hair loss.

- A tea made from steeping nettle leaves in boiling water is said to help those with hair problems.

- Coconut oil nourishes the scalp and helps rejuvenate the hair follicles. Gently massage the oil into the affected part of the scalp and continue this treatment for about a month.

- The pulp from green apples contains a polyphenol compound that has been found to promote hair growth. Apply the green apple extract as often as possible for a period of six months.

- Liquorice contains a compound that prevents the conversion of testosterone into DHT, so try adding some to your shampoo.

BELCHING

Belching or burping is the body's way of releasing trapped gas from the stomach. It often occurs when food or drink is taken too fast or in excess, and sometimes it is just a natural reaction to a certain type of food. Make sure you eat regularly and small amounts, and try any of the following to help keep gas at bay.

Treatment

- By having soup as a starter, it can often control excessive belching. Soup helps to prepare the stomach for the digestion process by getting rid of liquids and salts that generate gastric acid.

- Mint is very soothing if taken on an acid stomach, so add a few fresh mint leaves to some hot water and allow it to seep for a few minutes. It is a natural digestive agent and eases the digestive processes taking place inside the intestines and the stomach.

- Other herbal teas can help with belching, such as blackberry, raspberry, and chamomile.

- Drink a glass of water mixed with half a teaspoon of baking soda to get instant relief.

- Soak some fenugreek in hot water and drink early in the morning on an empty stomach.

- Lemon is perhaps one of the best home remedies for belching. Drink a cup of water mixed with two teaspoons of lemon juice and a small quantity of apple cider vinegar before eating. It helps to prevent the build-up of acid in the stomach and the formation of any unwanted gases.

BODY ODOUR

Some people suffer more than others with unpleasant body odour. This may be due to anxiety, your body reacting to strenuous physical exercise, or overheating. Most people can control body odour by using proprietary deodorants, but on certain people these can make the problem worse, particularly if the odour is due to a serious illness. If you suspect you have an underlying problem then it is essential you consult your doctor immediately. For those people who have a problem with body odour, make sure you are very careful with your personal hygiene and try only to wear clothes that are made out of natural fibres. Also, add turnip or turnip juice to your diet as it has been suggested that this will prevent the occurrence of body odour for up to ten hours.

Treatment

- Instead of using deodorant, try wiping your armpits with white vinegar.

- Apply some baking soda to the armpit as this will not only absorb the sweat but it will also kill the bacteria causing it.

- Avoid eating foods that contain refined sugar, white flour, hydrogenated oils, and any processed foods. Avoid eating red meat because this can release a lot of toxins into the bloodstream. Make sure you eat a healthy diet that contains plenty of whole grains, fresh leafy vegetables, fruits, and nuts.

- Drinking a cup of sage tea daily will reduce the activity of sweat glands and ultimately will minimize the odour.

- Add a tablespoon of liquid honey to your bathwater to help keep body odour in check. The water will feel silky soft and, believe it or not, will not leave your skin feeling sticky as you might imagine.

- Watch your coffee and tea intake by limiting yourself to two cups per day. Caffeine can stimulate the autonomic nervous system, which regulates sweating.

BODY RASH

Rashes can be unsightly and irritating, and very difficult to get rid of. It is generally an allergic reaction to a food or substance and it is the body's way of telling you that it doesn't like it. I know my skin reacts if I try to change my washing powder or soap, so I tend to stick to brands that are non-perfumed and suitable for use on young children. If you suspect the allergy could be due to something you have eaten, think carefully back over the last few days to see if you have changed your diet radically.

Treatment

- An oatmeal bath is effective in treating body rash as it relieves inflammation. Simply put a cup of uncooked oatmeal into your bath water and have a nice long soak. Make sure the water isn't too hot before getting in, otherwise this could aggravate the rash.

- Wash the affected areas with warm chamomile tea to soothe the itching.

- Aloe vera gel rubbed over the itchy parts can also bring relief.

BRONCHITIS

Bronchitis is an inflammation of the mucous membrane that lines the bronchial tubes situated inside the lungs. It can either be acute or chronic, if the latter then you must seek medical advice. The patient may experience a fever, difficulty in breathing, severe coughing and wheezing, and often a pain in the chest. Bronchitis can be caused by excessive smoking as the smoke irritates the bronchial tubes.

Treatment

- One of the most effective remedies for treating bronchitis is the use of turmeric powder. Add half a teaspoon to a glass of milk and drink two to three times a day.

- Pick some stinging nettles, leaving the roots intact, and grind them to a pulp in a pestle and mortar. Put the pulp in some muslin and squeeze out as much of the juice as possible. Mix the juice with some honey and take a couple of teaspoonfuls each day in a glass of warm water.

- Mix together half a teaspoon of ginger, pepper, and ground cloves. This can be licked with honey or taken as an infusion. The mixture of these three ingredients has antipyretic qualities which helps in lowering a fever.

- Raw onion has expectorant properties which help to break down phlegm. Either eat a few pieces of raw onion each day or take a teaspoonful of raw onion juice first thing in the morning.

- Eating plenty of garlic can help prevent bronchitis because it is filled with both antiviral and antibacterial properties.

- A hot bath containing a cup of Epsom salts is also beneficial. The patient should soak in the tub for at least 20 minutes. If the patient is experiencing chest pain, then hot towels applied to the upper chest can help relieve the discomfort.

- A healthy diet and plenty of fresh air are important when treating bronchitis. Try to take a walk every morning and follow it with a glass of fresh orange juice to build up your vitamin C intake.

COLD SORES

Cold sores are small blisters caused by the herpes simplex virus. They usually appear on the skin adjacent to the mouth or on the lips themselves. They are very contagious so try to avoid touching them or you could spread them to other parts of your face or to another person. Before the appearance of the blister, the patient will probably notice a tingling in the area, then a red or brown lesion will appear that will eventually burst and ooze. They are rather unsightly and can be quite an embarrassment to the victim. Cold sores are often the aftermath of the common cold, but they can also be triggered by any number of things such as pregnancy, gum or teeth problems, fatigue, stress, or hormonal changes. The virus can lay dormant under the skin and can reoccur if the patient becomes run down. Always wash your hands after touching the blisters and never share personal belongings such as your toothbrush or a face cloth with another person. Remember, kissing can spread the virus, too. Lysine – an essential amino acid – helps inhibit the spread of cold sores and can be found in red meat, milk, eggs, cheese, wheatgerm, and fish.

Treatment

- Ice is a very good home remedy for cold stores and should be applied to the skin for a few minutes once an hour.

- Press a warm teabag on the blister and hold in place for about ten minutes.

- Applying witch hazel, aloe vera gel, or common salt to the sore will give some relief.

● Avoid both salty foods and foods rich in acid. Your diet should include foods that contain vitamins A, C and E, zinc and iron. Eat plenty of fresh fruit and green leafy vegetables and include plenty of garlic in your diet.

● Lavender oil dabbed on the sores can also offer relief.

COMMON COLD

A common cold occurs more frequently than any other disease – hence its name. A person can suffer from a cold several times in one year and it can last from around three to ten days, leaving the person feeling miserable and run down. The initial signs of a cold are generally a sore throat and congestion of the nasal passages. The symptoms include a runny nose, sneezing, a slight rise in temperature, a headache, sore throat, various aches and pains in the body, and a general loss of appetite. Colds are spread very easily from person to person and because you are likely to come in contact with infected people on a regular basis, the best form of defence is to try and build up your immune system.

Treatment

● Lemon is beneficial in treating all types of cold with fever. It is rich in vitamin C which increases the body's resistance, decreases toxicity, and will help to reduce the duration of the cold. Squeeze the juice of one lemon into a glass of warm water and add a teaspoon of honey. Drink twice daily.

● Garlic soup (*see opposite page for my recipe*) is an old remedy which can help to reduce the severity of a cold. Garlic contains both anti-spasmodic and antiseptic properties, and the oil within the bulb also helps to open up the respiratory passages. If taken in the form of soup it will flush out toxins from the system and bring down fever.

Granny's Garlic Soup

You will need

7 cloves garlic, peeled
100 ml (3 fl oz) extra virgin olive oil
3 shallots, finely chopped
2 cloves
½ tsp hot smoked paprika
5 sprigs fresh thyme
2 bay leaves
12 cherry tomatoes, halved
1.5 litres (2¼ pints) chicken stock
    (this can be made by boiling the
    carcase when you next have
    roast chicken)
salt and freshly ground pepper

Method

1. Put the garlic cloves in a small saucepan and cover with extra virgin olive oil. Heat over a medium heat until the oil starts to bubble gently. Lower the heat and cook until the garlic is soft and then remove them using a slotted spoon.
2. Push the garlic through a sieve and put to one side.
3. Heat 1 tablespoon of the garlic-infused oil in a large saucepan and gently fry the shallots until they are soft. Add the reserved garlic purée, cloves, paprika, thyme, bay leaves, and tomatoes. Fry gently for a further five minutes, then pour in the chicken stock.
4. Simmer the soup for at least 30 minutes to allow the flavours to infuse thoroughly. You might like to add a little sherry vinegar to enhance the flavours.

- Ginger is another excellent remedy for both coughs and colds. Add about 10 grams (0.25 oz) of fresh ginger, cut up into small pieces, to a cup of warm water. Add either half a teaspoon of sugar or a teaspoon of honey and drink while still hot.

- If the patient has blocked nasal passages, a few drops of eucalyptus oil on a tissue or handkerchief can help open up the nostrils. Alternatively you can use a few drops in really hot water and use it as an inhalant by leaning over the bowl with a towel covering the head.

- The patient should get plenty of sleep, fresh air, and make sure they eat a healthy diet rich in vitamin C.

CONSTIPATION

I should imagine that everyone has suffered from constipation at least once in their life. If allowed to continue for more than a couple of days, the patient can start to feel quite unwell. The most common causes of constipation can be attributed to a poor diet, irregular eating habits, and an overindulgence in alcohol. By using natural remedies to cure constipation you are being kinder to your digestive system.

Treatment

- The easiest way to cure this condition is to change your diet so that it includes plenty of fibre and fresh fruit and vegetables – particularly grapes, prunes, raisins, figs, rhubarb, and pears.

- Increase your intake of wholegrain cereals, bran, honey, lentils, green and leafy vegetables.

- Avoid drinking tea as this is rich in tannins and helps to bind stools and hold back bowel movements which will make the condition even worse.

- Also avoid all products made of white flour, rice, bread, pulses, cakes, pastries, biscuits, cheese, white sugar, and hard-boiled eggs, all of which tend to bind you up.

- Avoid hurried meals and make sure you chew everything thoroughly.

- Exercise also plays an important role in the treatment of constipation, so make sure you get a walk in the fresh air every day or go swimming on a regular basis.

DANDRUFF

I am one of those fortunate people who have never suffered from this embarrassing complaint, and I believe it is mainly down to my healthy diet. The first sign of dandruff is when you see unsightly white flakes appear in the scalp and hair which are caused by a yeast-like fungus called malassezia. If left unchecked, it will lead to a mild inflammation that produces dead skin cells and leaves the scalp feeling itchy. These cells mix with the natural oils in your hair and clump together, making them appear white and flaky. Dandruff usually occurs when the person's general condition is low, at times of stress, incorrect diet, or overuse of harsh shampoos.

Treatment

- Soak two tablespoons of fenugreek seeds in water overnight and in the morning grind them to a fine paste. Rub the paste over the scalp and leave for half an hour before washing the hair in a mild shampoo.

- Using a teaspoon of fresh lime juice in the last rinse when washing your hair will not only make your hair really shiny, it will also prevent dandruff.

- Dab a dilute solution of apple cider vinegar on the scalp between shampooing, or add some to your final rinse.

- A hot steam bath is highly beneficial for both the hair and scalp. Massage hot oil and wrap a hot damp towel on the head for few minutes while soaking in the bath.

- Diet plays an important role in keeping your hair and scalp in good condition, so avoid eating citrus fruits, bananas, and tinned fruit, and avoid strong tea and coffee, pickles, and processed foods.

DARK CIRCLES UNDER THE EYES

Dark circles under the eyes can be unsightly and are often associated with lack of sleep or a sign of ill health. It may just be a hereditary problem or just a matter of getting older. As we age, our skin becomes dry and the dark circles become more prominent. Stress can also be a contributory factor as this usually means we are not getting a good night's sleep. Home remedies are by far the best way of tackling dark circles, as they will not do any harm to the skin or eyes.

Treatment

- Apply two thin slices of cucumber to each eye and leave in place for 15 to 20 minutes, while you relax. Do this twice a day and it will not only help to relieve the build-up of stress, but it also cools the eyes.

- Apply a mixture of honey and almond oil to the affected area every night before you go to bed. You should see a remarkable improvement in about three weeks.

- It is essential that you drink a lot of water as it helps to flush out any toxins that could be causing the dark circles.

- Make a paste out of fresh mint leaves with a few drops of lime juice added to it. Apply the paste to the affected area and leave on for about 15 minutes.

- Place a cold tea bag on top of each eye for 10 to 15 minutes every day.

- Rosewater is an old remedy that has been used for generations to help cool parts of the body. Apply two to three drops on a piece of cottonwool, and then use to gently massage the affected area for about five minutes.

- Make sure you eat a healthy diet, get at least eight hours of sleep a night, learn to relax, and make sure your skin stays clean and cool all the time so that it remains free of bacteria. Rather a tall order I know, but if you can manage all of these things your problem dark circles should go away.

DIARRHOEA

Diarrhoea is a common complaint particularly in children. Infectious diarrhoea – the more serious kind – is caused by viruses or bacteria, and needs to be treated by a medical practitioner. I am only dealing with the run-of-the-mill diarrhoea, here, which is caused by overeating, eating the wrong type of food, or a reaction to the use of a proprietary drug, as in the case of some antibiotics. Most people experience some diarrhoea when travelling, purely because our bodies are trying to cope with different conditions, bacteria, and foods. Make sure that you drink bottled water while on holiday if you are uncertain about the safety of drinking the local water, otherwise you could risk upsetting your stomach. Emotional stress and fright can also cause diarrhoea, but this usually only lasts for a short while. The most important thing when treating diarrhoea is to make sure the patient drinks plenty of fluids to avoid dehydration, as the body loses a lot of fluids and this in itself can cause secondary problems.

Treatment

- Buttermilk is very effective in treating diarrhoea, as the acid in the milk helps to fight germs and bacteria.

- Carrot soup is another good remedy because it not only replaces much of the water lost, but it also replenishes sodium, potassium, phosphorus, calcium, sulphur, and magnesium. It helps to stem the growth of harmful bacteria and prevents vomiting. The recipe is quite bland and is made by cooking half a kilogram (1 lb) of carrots in 150 ml (¼ pt) of water until they become soft. Liquidize the soup and add a small pinch of salt. Give a small amount of this soup to the patient every half an hour.

- Pectin is a soluble fibre that helps to add bulk to stools and soothes the stomach. Because apples are rich in pectin, eat plenty of pulp which should help stop the problem.

- Pomegranate seeds are beneficial in the treatment of diarrhoea because of their astringent properties. If the patient is getting weak from continuous purging, then give them about 50 ml of pomegranate juice to drink about once an hour.

In cases of severe diarrhoea starve the patient for a couple of days and only provide hot water to drink to replace the lost fluids. If it does not clear up after a couple of days, seek medical advice.

ECZEMA

Eczema is an irritating skin disorder, also called dermatitis. It usually occurs in infants and small children, but it is not uncommon for adults to suffer, too. The symptoms are itching, redness on the skin, dry and flaky skin, blisters, inflammation, and small bumps on the surface of the skin. It is not contagious and is thought to be hereditary, being closely linked to other conditions such as hay fever and asthma. Eczema can be aggravated by external irritants such as detergents, weather conditions, excessive heat, a deficiency in the vitamin B6, or emotional stress. The automatic response is to scratch the affected parts, but this only aggravates the condition, so it is important to find ways to relieve the itching.

Treatment

● Rub aloe vera gel directly onto the affected areas. If you have eczema on your scalp use an aloe vera shampoo daily.

● Tea tree oil is good at clearing up eczema patches by relieving the itching and swelling. It can be applied directly to the skin or added to a non-perfumed lotion to relieve dry skin.

● To help relieve the constant itching and help soften the dry skin of eczema, take a bath containing some oatmeal. As this can be quite messy, simply tie some oatmeal in a piece of muslin and let it circulate in the warm bath water. Do not use any soaps or cleansers and apply some aloe vera gel after drying off.

FEVER

Fever is usually the body's response to an underlying problem and is the way by which it eliminates bacteria and viruses. The most common symptom of fever is a rise in body temperature, but in severe cases it can be accompanied by sweating, dehydration, headache, muscle aches, loss of appetite, general weakness, and shivering. If the patient's temperature goes above 102°F, this can cause hallucinations, confusion, and irritability and you should seek medical advice immediately. The body temperature is regulated by the hypothalamus which is located at the base of the brain. If the body is trying to fight off an illness, the hypothalamus sets the temperature to try and rid the body of the unwanted disease. As soon as you realize the patient has a temperature, make sure they drink plenty of water to replenish the lost fluid. It is also a good idea to try and reduce the temperature and you can do this in several ways. Willow bark is an ancient natural remedy which the Greek physicians used to reduce fever and soothe pain. It is often referred to as nature's aspirin as they both contain salicylic acid. Anyone who has an allergic reaction to aspirin, therefore should not use willow.

Treatment

- Red peppers, cinnamon, and cranberries all have a source of salicylates which act to bring down the fever.

- Brew willow bark tea and drink it by taking small sips – but remember, it has an aspirin-related compound.

- For a mild fever crush 10 grams of raisins and 10 grams of fresh ginger. Boil them in 200 ml of water until it is reduced to a quarter of the original liquid. Strain and drink while still warm.

- Just drinking plenty of chilled water will have the effect of bringing down a slightly raised temperature.

- Only eat foods that are highly digestible and if your appetite is diminished, then stick to soups, yogurts, and other liquid foods.

- Avoid any strenuous exercise for a few days and try to remain in a constant temperature. Avoid heavy or fried foods until you feel better – in fact it would be better to avoid them anyway.

Granny's Best Cold and Flu Remedy

When I was growing up, granny always said that the best thing to eat when you were feeling ill was a hearty bowl of chicken soup. Apparently, this is not as silly as it sounds. It has been proved to have many therapeutic effects and it tastes marvellous as well.

You will need
one 2 to 2.5 kg (5 to 6 lb) chicken
3 large onions
1 large sweet potato
3 parsnips
2 turnips
10 large carrots
6 celery stems
1 bunch of parsley
salt and pepper to taste

Method
1. Clean the chicken thoroughly, put it in a large, heavy-based pot and cover with cold water. Bring the water to the boil.
2. Add the onions, sweet potato, parsnips, turnips, and carrots and boil for about 1½ hours.
3. Remove any fat that has accumulated on the surface of the stock and then add the celery and parsley. Cook for a further 45 minutes.
4. Remove the chicken and then put the liquid through a liquidizer, making sure you have removed all the bones first. Add salt and pepper to taste and feed to your patient with a lovely piece of fresh brown bread if their appetite is up to it.

GASTRITIS

Gastritis causes discomfort in the region of the stomach and is usually accompanied by a loss of appetite, nausea, vomiting (in severe cases), headache, and dizziness. Sometimes the patient may complain of heartburn or a feeling of being bloated shortly after eating. Gastritis is usually associated with poor dietary habits, such as overeating or continually eating the wrong type of food. Prolonged worry and tension can also cause gastritis, as well as the use of certain drugs.

Treatment

● Water from the centre of a coconut is an excellent remedy for gastritis. Fast for 24 hours, drinking small amounts at regular intervals. This will give the stomach the necessary rest and also provides essential vitamins and minerals.

● Potato juice is also beneficial in curing gastritis. The recommended dose is half a cup of juice, two to three times daily, half an hour before meals.

● Make a tea from dried marigold flowers as it is an ideal healing drink. Drink the tea twice a day, while it is nice and warm.

● In severe cases, the patient should fast a day and should only drink warm water during this period. This should flush out any toxins and allow the inflammation to subside.

● Rest a hot water bottle on the stomach either when empty or two hours after a meal to help ease the pain.

● Once the patient is on the mend, yogurt and cottage cheese are ideal foods to start with, until they have built themselves up to eating a normal, healthy diet. Try to avoid taking rushed meals;

the more relaxed the atmosphere, the better chance you have of making a quick recovery.

GINGIVITIS

Gingivitis is bleeding of the gums which is usually due to bad oral hygiene. If you suspect you have gingivitis, make an appointment to see your dentist. If not treated in time it can lead to more serious gum problems which could result in you losing some teeth. The early stages of gum disease are not usually painful, so you may not be aware that you have it. Some of the symptoms to look out for are painful gums, bleeding while brushing, red gums, swollen gums, bad breath, or a bad taste in the mouth. Sometimes gingivitis can be brought on by hormonal changes as in pregnancy or puberty, or by a poor diet, or taking a specific medication.

Treatment

- Gargle twice a day using a saline solution of half a teaspoon of salt in a glass of lukewarm water.

- Rub your gums with oil of cloves.

- Make a mouthwash using peppermint oil or chamomile to help soothe the gums.

- Your diet should be rich in fibre and vitamin C. Avoid sugary foods, fruit juices, white flour, white rice, soft drinks, and syrups. Eat plenty of fresh fruit and vegetables and avoid food that contains a lot of unhealthy fat.

HAEMORRHOIDS

Haemorrhoids or, as we old folk call them, piles are a swelling of the veins that are located in the anus and lower rectum. They develop from too much pressure being put on the veins, usually in the case of passing a hard stool or following childbirth. Haemorrhoids can be very painful or at times devoid of any symptoms at all. The symptoms themselves can differ as they can be either internal or external. Sometimes you are not aware you have internal haemorrhoids until you bleed when passing stools. External haemorrhoids often cause irritation and general discomfort in the anal region and cause pain when passing stools. They are usually visible as a sensitive lump. Diet can play a large part in preventing haemorrhoids as constipation is one of the primary causes. Obesity is also another contributary factor, so try to eat healthily and include plenty of fibre in your diet. Stay physically active with light activities such as walking, swimming, or cycling. Remember the only real cure for haemorrhoids is to prevent them – change your lifestyle and avoid constipation at all costs.

Treatment

- Boil the peel from a pomegranate in some water. Strain, and drink the water while still warm, twice a day.

- Eat some figs for breakfast that have been soaked overnight in water.

- Moisten some powdered comfrey with a little vegetable oil and apply the paste to the affected area.

- Witch hazel is a soothing, cooling astringent that can help relieve the pain and itching of haemorrhoids.

- Apply some aloe vera gel to the affected area to soothe the itching.

- Regular warm baths may relieve the irritation and help to keep the sensitive area clean.

> **CAUTION**
> If you continue to have excessive bleeding when passing stools, seek medical advice as it could be an underlying symptom of another digestive disease.

HANGOVERS

A hangover is referred to medically as veisalgia, and is caused by an overindulgence of alcoholic beverages. The symptoms are not very pleasant and being a teetotaller myself, I fail to understand how people can constantly put themselves through such purgatory. The mouth is generally very dry, the person will have the headache from hell and sometimes the head throbs so that any loud noise becomes uncomfortable. They often feel drowsy, have bloodshot eyes, and dislike exposure to bright lights. The stomach is very nauseous and this is often accompanied by bouts of vomiting. The dry mouth and headache result from the dehydration caused by ethyl alcohol, so the sufferer will need to drink plenty of water to rehydrate and flush out the toxins. If you know you are going to consume a lot of alcohol, such as at Christmas or New Year, then it is worth keeping a few handy hangover tips close by, because you won't feel like searching for them the following morning and you certainly won't remember them! See page 54 for one of my hangover cures.

Treatment

- If you are still *compos mentis* when you get home, try to remember to drink plenty of water before going to bed. Hopefully this will provide some relief from the effects of dehydration the next morning. If you can stomach it, also drink a lot of water when waking up.

- Try to make sure you don't drink on an empty stomach. If you can eat a meal before drinking, this helps to reduce the rate the alcohol enters your bloodstream and can assist in reducing the after-effects.

- Take some vitamin C tablets as these will help to break down the alcohol content in your body. Alternatively, eat some fruit that is rich in vitamin C.

- More sensibly – try to limit yourself to one drink an hour, or alternate your alcoholic drinks with water or non-alcoholic beverages. Try to avoid carbonated drinks though as these can speed up the absorption of alcohol.

- Bananas give you sugar, in the form of fructose, and potassium, which is one of the things you lose lots of when you drink. Bananas are also a natural antacid to help with the nausea, and are high in magnesium which can help relax those pounding blood vessels causing that hangover headache.

HAY FEVER

Hay fever is an allergic reaction which can be triggered by pollen, household dust, and other allergens present in the air throughout the year. Spring is the main season for hay fever and symptoms can include coughing, headache, itchy nose and eyes, sore throat, stuffy nose, and sneezing. Hay fever is caused when the airborne allergens enter our bodies and our immune system reacts to try and flush the pollen out of the airways. As we produce antibodies to fight the allergens our bodies produce histamine which causes the irritation.

Treatment
- Buy some local honey and add to boiled grapefruit and lemon juice. Take this solution three times a day. (Local honey is recommended because the allergy may be to a specific pollen. If

the honey contains some quantity of that pollen, then eating the honey little and often can help desensitize the body.)

- To stop irritation inside your nose, apply a little petroleum jelly.

- Add some eucalyptus oil to boiling water and use as a steam inhalation.

- Pollen is released in the early morning, keep windows closed at night so that pollen doesn't enter the house.

- Eat a diet rich in vitamin C and avoid flour, sugar, salt, and dairy products for one week. Drink plenty of water and herbal teas.

- Try to avoid going out early in the morning or late in the evening as these are the times the pollen count is at its highest.

HEADACHES

People are always searching for a quick solution to headaches, as they are one of the most common ailments people suffer from. Most headaches are caused by temporary upsets to the system and they are nature's way of warning you that there is something wrong. The pain itself arises from an irritation to nerve endings in the shoulders, neck, and muscles in the scalp. Many prescription analgesics come either directly from plants or a chemical imitation, so using herbs to take the pain away is not as silly as it sounds. Normal headaches are annoying but they are usually easy to treat, especially if you can learn to relax and take the stress out of your body. Unfortunately, there is a percentage of the population who suffer from debilitating migraines, which can last for several hours or days and are much harder to treat. I am a sufferer myself and know just how much they can affect your life – see page 95 for help with migraine.

Treatment

- Drink black tea that contains three or four slices of lemon.

- Marjoram works well for treating a nervous headache. Make an infusion of the leaves and drink as a tea.

- Make a steam inhalation by boiling several sprigs of rosemary in water. Cover the head with a towel and breathe in the vapour for as long as possible. Repeat until the headache is relieved.

- Eating raw red pepper can also be a good pain reliever as it contains aspirin-like salicylates.

HEARTBURN

Heartburn is a very common complaint and it is estimated that at least 30 per cent of the adult population experience it at least once a month. Heartburn is caused when the gastric acid in the stomach refluxes back to the oesophagus. The patient usually experiences a burning sensation or pain in the chest/stomach region shortly after eating. It can often occur when you lie down following a meal. Heartburn is usually triggered by bad eating habits, such as eating a meal too quickly or failing to chew the food sufficiently. Fried foods, hot and spicy foods, sugar, alcohol, cigarettes, and coffee have all been associated with heartburn, so if you are a regular sufferer you might like to rethink your lifestyle.

Treatment

- Make sure you eat regularly and try not to skip any meals as this allows the acid to build up. Drink plenty of water, eat slowly, and never go to bed or lie down immediately after a meal.

- A glass of chilled milk is a quick remedy for heartburn.

- If you feel that acid is building up in your stomach, chew on a few basil leaves.

- Chew a few almonds when you feel heartburn coming on.

- Ginger root mixed with some honey after a meal can help prevent the build-up of acid.

- Drink some chamomile or mint tea to help soothe the burning sensation.

HICCUPS

Hiccups come from the diaphragm, a dome-shaped muscle in the chest. The diaphragm is responsible for pushing and pulling air in and out of the lungs and if it becomes irritated for any reason, it causes hiccups. As the diaphragm contracts it causes a 'hic' sound in the throat, which can be very annoying, especially if you are in the middle of an important meeting. Generally, hiccups will only last for a few minutes, but they have been known to last for days or weeks. If your hiccups do not subside after 12 hours, contact your doctor as it could be a sign of some other medical problem in your body. You will probably have been told many different ways of curing hiccups, such as holding your breath, drinking out of the wrong side of the glass, giving someone a fright – or a heart attack more likely! – or drinking a glass of soda water as fast as you can. I can't say that any of these have worked for me, but the one positive cure I have found is that if you drink a glass of water and exaggerate the swallowing action several times, the hiccups will be gone in no time.

Treatment

● Alternatively, try putting a sugar lump on the end of your tongue and leaving it there until it has dissolved.

● Get a glass of lukewarm water and place a clean piece of muslin over the top. Drink the water through the cloth and, hey presto, the hiccups have gone!

HIGH CHOLESTEROL

In my day no one ever mentioned cholesterol and we went on enjoying all the luxuries that were denied us during the war without giving our bodies a second thought. Today, the importance of cholesterol is drummed into us constantly, but what exactly is it? Cholesterol is a yellowish, fatty substance, which, despite its bad press, is an essential ingredient of the body. Although it is essential to life, it also has a bad reputation for being a major contributory factor in heart disease. Most of the cholesterol produced in the body comes from the liver, but did you know that nearly 30 per cent is produced by the food we eat? There are two different types of cholesterol or lipoproteins – a low-density one called LDL and a high-density one called HDL. Amazingly, it is LDL that is considered to be the one that carries the greatest risk. Although much of cholesterol build-up is due to our genes, you are increasing the risk by eating rich and fried foods, and excessive amounts of dairy products such as butter and cream. Pastries, biscuits, cakes, cheese, and ice cream, as well as smoking and drinking, all play a contributory factor. Stress is also a major cause of increased levels of cholesterol, so learning to relax is very important.

A fatty substance called lecithin can help to break up unwelcome cholesterol into smaller particles so that the body can handle it efficiently. There are foods that are rich in lecithin and they should be regular ingredients in your diet – egg yolk, vegetable oils, wholegrain cereals, soyabeans, and unpasteurized milk. Sunflower seeds are another valuable product in reducing cholesterol, as they contain a substantial quantity of linoleic acid which helps to break down fatty deposits on the walls of arteries. Foods high in soluble fibre can also help your body avoid high LDL levels. Soluble fibre can be found in such foods as oats, oranges, pears, brussels sprouts, and carrots.

Treatment

- A daily snack of two raw carrots will significantly lower your levels of bad cholesterol.

- Although avocado is one of the highest fat-containing fruits, it has been found to be beneficial in reducing LDL.

- Beans are high in fibre and low in fat, so these should be a regular part of your diet.

- Try to eat at least one clove of garlic a day.

- Keep your diet full of fibre by eating wheat bran, wholegrain cereals, potatoes, carrots, beetroot, turnips, mangoes, and guavas, as well as leafy vegetables such as cabbage, lettuce, and celery.

- Try to drink at least six glasses of water each day. Water is also beneficial to people who suffer from high blood pressure as it helps the kidneys excrete toxins, which in turn elimates excessive cholesterol from the system.

- Make sure you take plenty of exercise, as it not only plays a vital role in lowering LDL but also improves circulation.

HIVES (OR URTICARIA)

Hives is a nasty little rash that appears on the skin when you come into contact with an allergen that your system doesn't like. Your skin can swell and is usually covered with little red rings or patches which itch like crazy. A classic example of hives is nettle rash, but just about anything can cause hives, from certain foods or animal contact, to plants and even some drugs. In severe cases, the patient might experience difficulty in breathing and swallowing and feel dizzy or faint; in such extreme cases you should always seek medical advice immediately. If possible, you need to be able to identify what has caused the hives so that it can be avoided in future, but this is sometimes easier said than done. I suffered from an itchy rash around my neck which kept coming back from time to time. I eventually tracked it down to a hairspray I used, but only on special occasions when I put on my glad rags!

Treatment

- This might sound ironic, seeing as nettles can give you hives, but if you dry the roots and make an infusion to drink, it will quickly get rid of the problem. A few teaspoons of dried nettle leaves made into a tea also works well.

- Of course the old favourite calamine lotion is great for reducing the itching associated with hives.

- To stop the itching fill a bath with warm water and add half a cup of cornflour and half a cup of baking soda. Soak yourself for at least 15 minutes once a day.

- Because stress can trigger hives, even in the absence of allergies, it is important to try and keep all forms of stress out of your lives if at all possible. I can recommend retirement, it works wonders!

- Try dabbing milk of magnesia on the lesions. As this is an alkaline solution it helps remove some of the irritating sensation.

- Applying aloe vera gel directly to the affected area can quickly help the allergy to subside.

INDIGESTION

I don't suppose there are many people who haven't experienced the discomfort of indigestion at some time or another. Also known as dyspepsia, it is similar to heartburn in that it is due to excess stomach acid which can irritate the oesophagus. The symptoms include stomach ache, nausea, bloating of the stomach, uncontrolled burping, heartburn, flatulence, and acid regurgitation. Any number of things can trigger indigestion including eating too fast, rich food, smoking, drinking, stress, and anxiety to name but a few. It is easy to treat and will usually subside very quickly if nipped in the bud.

Treatment

- To prevent acid indigestion put some lemon juice or cider vinegar in a glass of water and drink it before a heavy meal.

- Drink some water containing a few drops of peppermint essence every three to four hours.

- Instead of coffee, drink ginger tea after a meal as this helps the body digest food more quickly.

- Chamomile tea is very effective in soothing the gut.

- For instant relief take a glass of honey and lemon juice, both mixed in equal quantity in some warm water, then add a teaspoon of baking soda.

- Take small and frequent meals and avoid going straight to bed after eating. Avoid drinks that contain caffeine and try not to eat too much chocolate.

- Avoid wearing clothes that are too tight around your stomach, and try and decrease your levels of stress.

- Regular exercise is also very good for the digestive system.

IRRITABLE BOWEL SYNDROME (IBS)

I used to have a mild form of IBS, but discovered as long as I didn't drink white coffee after a meal I was fine. The symptoms of IBS can vary from person to person. For some it just comes and goes away, as in my case, but for those more unfortunate people it can be a constant problem. The primary symptoms include bloating, abdominal pain, and general discomfort followed sometimes by a bout of diarrhoea. If you are lucky enough to know what triggers a bout, then the food can be avoided. If, however, you cannot find a common denominator, then you are less fortunate and may need to consider seeking medical advice for a more permanent solution.

Treatment

- Take a few drops of peppermint essence in warm water to help alleviate the cramping sensation.

- Herbs such as chamomile, valerian, rosemary, and lemon balm are all effective due to their antispasmodic properties.

- Drink ginger tea or eat raw ginger to reduce inflammation.

- Avoid carbonated drinks and drink at least six to eight glasses of water each day.

- Try to avoid caffeine and eat fresh fruit and vegetables and plenty of fibre. Fibre improves the performance of the intestines and helps to stabilize the symptoms.

- Eat small meals regularly and try to avoid any large meals just before going to bed. Exercise regularly and try to destress your life.

LARYNGITIS

Laryngitis takes me back to the time when I was bridesmaid at my best friend's wedding, at the tender age of 18. I was fine until the day of the wedding, when I woke up with a voice that sounded more like a frog trying to croak than a human talking. I had no other symptoms, but I was devastated as I had written a comical speech which I was looking forward to delivering. Of course I made the wedding, but the speech was read out by the best man which somehow didn't sound quite right as it was full of little girlie anecdotes. True laryngitis, not to be confused with a sore throat, is hoarseness or loss of voice due to the swelling of the larynx or voice box. The most common cause is an upper respiratory infection such as a common cold, or it can be due to overuse or abuse of the voice such as yelling or shouting for a prolonged period of time. Singers often suffer from laryngitis if they do not give their vocal cords time to recover. Staying hydrated will help to speed your recovery, so make sure you drink plenty of fluids.

Treatment

- Gargle several times a day with a solution of warm water containing half a teaspoon of salt. Do not be tempted to add more salt as this can aggravate the problem.

- Gargle with white vinegar and water in equal amounts, two to three times a day, as viruses and bacteria do not like an acidic environment.

- Extract the juice from a lemon and add a pinch of salt. Mix one teaspoon of the lemon concentrate into a glass of warm water and gargle as needed.

- Drinking a tea with ginger and honey will also help soothe the soreness in the throat. It is important to keep the throat moist, so remember to drink plenty of water as well.

LEG CRAMPS

Cramp and old age seem to go hand in hand, but having said that, there are many young people and sportsmen and women who suffer as well. It is an involuntary contraction of a muscle or muscles in the leg, which is excruciatingly painful and very distressing if it happens in the middle of the night. It usually occurs in the calf muscle or the hamstring, and can last from less than a minute to several minutes at a time. Cramp will often rear its ugly head when you inadvertently stretch your leg out in bed and you are woken up with a searing pain and a hard lump in the back of your leg. It can be caused by dehydration, rigorous exercise (although not in my case these days!), a diminished blood supply, or a lack of certain nutrients in the body.

What to do when you get leg cramps

- Stretch the leg out straight, even if it kills you to do it, pointing the toes upwards towards the head. Then massage the cramped muscle gently in the natural direction of the muscle. This should help to relax the contraction and ease the pain.

- If you are finding it hard to relax the muscle, then taking a warm shower or bath should help.

- Alternatively, use cold packs on the affected muscle to release the tension.

- Increase water consumption to stay well hydrated during the day.

- Eat foods that are rich in both potassium (e.g. apricot, banana, baked potato) and calcium (e.g. dairy products, lettuce, broccoli, beans, and almonds).

- If you regularly get cramps during the night, try sleeping with a rolled up blanket or pillow under your feet to prevent you from pointing your toes downwards while you are asleep.

- Make sure you stretch before starting and finishing an exercise routine and drink plenty of fluids during and after your workout.

- If you are lucky enough to have a static bicycle at home, pedalling for a few minutes before you go to bed should stop the night cramps.

MIGRAINE

I mentioned migraines briefly under the heading 'headaches', but any sufferer will know that they come under a totally different category. Some migraine sufferers will tell you that they get warning signs such as flashing lights, blurred vision or an extreme tiredness, while others will tell you that they come upon you without giving you time to take preventative action. The headache associated with migraine is usually on one side of the head, or very often behind the eyes, but the pain can become so severe that the patient is unable to tell you exactly where the source is located. Migraine headaches often occur after a period of overwork or continuous stress, because the patient suddenly relaxes the tight muscles which allows them to expand and stretch the walls of the blood vessels. The blood pumped with each heartbeat then pushes the vessels further causing intense pain. Many people have reported that their senses seem to be particularly acute and are unable to stand loud noises, bright lights, or strong smells. It can also be accompanied by loss of appetite, nausea or vomiting, and on occasion numbness or weakness of an arm or leg. Early symptoms are often irritability, lethargy, stiff neck, incessant yawning, and confused thinking.

Treatment

● Obtain the juice from really ripe grapes and drink neat.

● Niacin has proved helpful in relieving migraine pain, and it can be found naturally in whole wheat, green leafy vegetables, tomatoes, nuts, sunflower seeds, liver, and fish.

● Watch your diet carefully to see if you can find out what triggers the migraine. Adopt a well-balanced diet and make sure you drink plenty of water.

● If you know your migraines are stress-related, then try relaxing techniques such as yoga or just take some quiet time for yourself at least once a day to unwind.

● Make sure you exercise regularly and get plenty of fresh air; walking will help to relieve the tension.

● If a migraine is in full flow, get some kind soul to put a cold compress on your forehead with a few drops of lavender oil added and warm towels on the back of your neck.

OBESITY

Obesity is a physical condition that results from too much fat being stored in the body. We need to store a certain amount of fat to reserve our energy levels, but an excess can result in obesity and other major health disorders, such as type 2 diabetes, high blood pressure, osteoarthritis, high cholesterol, and many others besides. Do not be mistaken that obesity and being overweight are the same thing. The latter refers to an increase in weight of the total body whereas obesity refers to excessive fat tissue only. It is the result of eating more food than the body needs, can occur at any age, and affects both sexes. Obesity is a major health hazard as it puts extra strain on the heart, kidneys, liver, and joints. To rid the body of obesity, the patient needs to rethink their lifestyle completely. Instead of leading a sedentary life and eating exactly what they fancy, they need to gradually build up a regular form of exercise and start taking what they eat seriously. Before embarking on any drastic changes, the patient should consult a medical practitioner, who will be able to give them some dietary guidelines. If you are really serious about losing that excess weight, then you might like to think carefully about what causes your overeating.

A helping hand to losing weight

- Honey is great at helping kickstart the system into losing some weight. One teaspoon of honey mixed with the juice of half a lime in a glass of lukewarm water can be drunk on a regular basis instead of a can of fizzy drink or a tea and coffee packed with sugar.

- Mint is also beneficial in dealing with problems associated with obesity. Drink mint tea whenever you fancy a hot drink.

- Substitute a rich milkshake with a regular intake of carrot juice.

- To control the urge to eat, boil fresh ginger in a pot and add some slices of lemon. Drink while still warm to stop those cravings.

- Avoid the intake of too much salt as this could be a factor for increasing body weight.

- Avoid any foods that are high in fat.

- One or two ripe tomatoes eaten early in the morning as a substitute for breakfast for a couple of months is considered to be a safe method of losing weight.

- Avoid high calorie foods such as chocolates, cakes, biscuits, sweets, and ice cream.

- Never skip a meal, and eat little and often so that you never feel too hungry.

- Drink a glass of boiled water after every meal to help fill you up.

- Make sure you eat slowly and chew each morsel of food many times, so that your body is tricked into thinking it has had more than it actually has.

- Start a gentle exercise routine by walking and avoid any negative thoughts. Keep your mind and your body busy and then you won't need to think about food.

Choosing healthy foods that satiate your hunger is a great way to lose weight and to keep it off forever. Avoid foods that are high in calories, for instance salted peanuts, and go for ones that contain water and dietary fibre. Two prime examples of this are carrots and grapefruit. When you want a special treat, try granny's wholemeal muffins on the next page, which are low in fat, high in fibre, and will give you that satisfied feeling. With the whole grains and dried fruits, these muffins contain a variety of healthy antioxidants and fibre. I apologize now for the recipe using cup measurements, but this delicious recipe was given to me by my sister who lives in Connecticut, USA, and I don't know how to convert it accurately. Cup measures are easy to buy in the UK and I always keep a set in my kitchen drawer for times like this.

US Granny's Appetite Busters

You will need   *Makes 12*

1 cup whole wheat flour (about 135 g/4¾ oz)
¼ cup packed brown sugar
2 tablespoons untoasted wheat germ
2 tablespoons wheat bran
1½ teaspoons baking soda
1 teaspoon ground cinnamon
½ teaspoon salt
1½ cups quick-cooking oats
⅓ cup chopped dates
⅓ cup raisins
⅓ cup dried cranberries
1 cup low-fat buttermilk
¼ cup vegetable oil
1 teaspoon vanilla essence
1 large egg, lightly beaten
½ cup boiling water

Method

1. Sift the flour and other dry ingredients into a large bowl and mix well. Stir in oats, dates, raisins, and cranberries.
2. Combine the buttermilk, oil, vanilla, and lightly beaten egg. Make a well in the centre of the flour mixture and add the liquid. Stir until all the ingredients are combined.
3. Stir in the boiling water and leave the batter to stand for 15 minutes.
4. Preheat the oven to 375°F/190°C/gas mark 5. Spoon the batter into lightly greased muffin tins and cook until the muffins spring back when touched lightly in the centre.

PALPITATIONS

Although I have never suffered from palpitations myself, I remember a good friend of mine who experienced them for the first time and just how frightened she was. She had just received some dreadful news and the shock caused her heart to race uncontrollably and she said she could actually feel the thumping of her heart in her chest. The vast majority of cases are due to anxiety, overeating, or sometimes just the fact that the person is lying on their left side which means the heart is nearer to the chest wall. In the majority of cases it is more distressing than serious, but sometimes it can indicate a more serious condition so it is worth speaking to your doctor about it before embarking on any natural remedies.

Treatment

- Grapes are one of the most effective natural remedies for heart palpitations. Drink grape juice at frequent intervals.

- Eat a ripe guava daily on an empty stomach. This is particularly beneficial if the disorder is caused by nervousness or anaemia.

- Drink a warm glass of water containing a tablespoon of honey and the juice of half a lemon just before going to bed.

- Try to stick to a light diet that contains a lot of fresh fruit and raw or lightly cooked vegetables.

- Avoid tea, coffee, alcohol, cigarettes, fizzy drinks, and any foods that contain artificial colourings or chemical additives. Try to eat regularly and only take small amounts at each helping.

- Try to learn the art of relaxation and make sure you take some exercise daily, such as a brisk walk, cycling, or swimming.

PSORIASIS

Psoriasis is a stubborn disease that produces red, irritated skin with bright silvery scales. It is not contagious but can be very unsightly and irritating. The areas that psoriasis usually attacks are the elbows, knees and the skin behind the ears, the trunk, and the scalp. The lesions themselves are always dry and can vary in size quite considerably. Psoriasis does seem to run in families and can be aggravated by stress, infections, and some proprietary medications that upset the natural balance of the body.

Treatment

- One of the most effective home remedies for psoriasis is cabbage leaves. Use the thick outer leaves, which should be washed in warm water and then dried with paper towel. The leaves should then be flattened, softened, and smoothed out by rolling them with a heavy rolling pin. Gently warm the leaves and then lay them over the top of the affected area. Put a soft elastic bandage over the top to hold them in place.

- Drink buttermilk on a regular basis. You can also apply buttermilk as a compress to the affected area to speed up the healing process.

- Mashed avocado applied to the affected parts is very soothing and helps clear up the skin.

- Brazil nuts contain selenium and are also rich in vitamin E. If you are able to get hold of some oil apply it to the affected areas.

- Try to avoid animal fats including milk, butter, and eggs and embark on a diet of fresh fruit, whole grains, and raw or lightly cooked vegetables. Avoid tea and coffee and drink plenty of water to flush out the system.

- Take a hot bath that contains some Epsom salts to help relieve the itching. After the bath apply a little olive oil to the skin, but make sure you dry in all the creases first.

SINUSITIS

This is something that I am only too familiar with as my husband has a constant battle with his sinuses. Sinusitis can often follow a common cold or other general infection which allows germs to find their way into the sinuses or the chambers on either side of the nasal passage. The symptoms usually include constant sneezing, headaches, a runny and blocked nose, and an uncomfortable pressure around the head, eyes, and face.

Treatment

- Cut out mucus-forming foods and common allergic foods, such as dairy products, eggs, wheat, fried and fatty foods, pastries, sugar, chocolate, beer, and anything containing food additives.

- Eat more sinus-clearing foods, which aid the breakdown of mucus. These include fresh fruit and vegetables, salads, fish, and hot chicken broth. Foods that are known to be particularly beneficial are garlic, onions, chillies, ginger, horseradish, mustard, and pineapple.

- Drink a glass of carrot juice daily. To make it more interesting you can always add some extra ingredients like ginger and apple.

- Make a steam inhalation by adding a few drops of eucalyptus oil to a bowl of really hot water.

- Garlic and onions are very beneficial in treating sinusitis. Start with small doses and gradually build up your intake.

- Mangoes have a high concentration of vitamin A which contributes towards the formation of healthy epithelium, or the cells that line the sinus.

- Avoid using perfumes or any strongly scented cosmetics which can aggravate the sinuses.

TONSILLITIS

A few years ago doctors believed the only cure for tonsillitis was to have the tonsils removed, as in the case of my older sister who suffered frequently with sore throats as a young child. Today, they are not so quick to whip them out, as they now believe the tonsils actually help the nose and throat fight off infections. Tonsillitis is when the tonsils become inflamed due to either a bacterial or viral infection. The symptoms usually include a sore throat, hoarse voice, visibly red and swollen tonsils, tender lymph glands in the neck, a fever, headache, ear ache, and a burning in the back of the throat.

Treatment

- Squeeze some fresh lime into a glass of warm water, add four teaspoons of honey and a pinch of salt and sip slowly.

- Drink a glass of pure, boiled milk containing a pinch of turmeric powder every night for three nights.

- Simmer two tablespoons of fenugreek seeds in a litre of water for about half an hour and then leave to cool. Gargle regularly and throw away any liquid at the end of the day as it will not keep.

- Drink a juice of carrot, beetroot, and cucumber, either as a combination or individually. The proportion recommended is 300 ml (11 fl oz) of carrot juice to 100 ml (3 fl oz) of beetroot and cucumber.

- Gargle with warm salt water – one teaspoon to a small glass – every few hours to relieve symptoms.

- Feed the patient some ice cream or soothing sorbet to help ease the burning at the back of the throat.

TOENAIL FUNGUS

Fungal infections under the nails of both the toes and fingers are common and known medically as onychomycosis. It is a contagious and unsightly infection which causes disfiguration and discoloration of the nails. The affected nail will become yellow or brown in colour and you may find that the area can have quite a foul smell. The nail itself can become very thick and overgrown which makes the wearing of shoes rather painful. It is possible to pick up the fungus in damp areas such as public gyms, shared showers, or swimming baths. Try not to wear tight socks or shoes for a long period of time, because moist, warm conditions are the perfect environment for fungal growth. Also make sure you dry your feet carefully after bathing or swimming, so that there are no damp areas when you put your shoes back on.

Treatment

- Tea tree oil is a potent natural antiseptic and fungicide, so apply it undiluted to the affected nail.

- Soak your toenails for 15 to 20 minutes in a bowl full of warm water and natural apple cider vinegar mixed in equal proportion. Make sure you dry your feet thoroughly afterwards.

- Oil of oregano has antiseptic, antibacterial, antiparasitical, antiviral, analgesic, and antifungal properties. Blend two drops of this essential oil with a teaspoon of olive oil and apply to the affected nail daily. Do not use for longer than three weeks.

- Put an equal amount of tea tree oil and lavender oil on a piece of cotton wool and dab it under the toe nail and surrounding area two or three times a day.

- As with many conditions, diet plays a vital role in the control of fungal infections. Try to include foods that contain probiotics, such as yogurt and yogurt drinks, as these will help to build up the good bacteria in your system.

VARICOSE VEINS

I am one of the lucky ones who do not suffer from unsightly veins on their legs and I am still quite happy to expose mine in skirts that are probably far too short for my advancing years. Those people who do, usually feel uncomfortable about baring their legs to the world, so if we can offer them some relief without having to go through painful surgery, then so much the better. Varicose veins occur when the valves in the veins themselves don't work properly. This means that blood forms little pools which subsequently leak blood and fluid into the surrounding tissue. The first sign of a varicose vein is usually a swelling along the course of the vein, which can then be followed by muscular cramps. They can be the result of factors such as constant constipation, lack of exercise, smoking, obesity, standing for long periods of time, or wearing clothing that is too tight – all of which contribute to a sluggish circulation. Many women suffer this complaint in the early years of childbearing, as the pressure in the pelvis and abdomen can slow down the flow of blood to the lower extremities.

Treatment
- Violet flowers contain large amounts of a compound called rutun, which can help build up the strength of the capillary walls. If you don't mind munching on these scented little flowers, then you will find eating a few a day can provide you with enough rutun.

- Marigold is very beneficial in treating varicose veins. A compress of the flowers should be applied externally to help with inflamed or ulcerated skin.

- Raw vegetable juice, especially carrot, should be included in the diet.

- Lemon peel contains substances known as flavonoids, including rutin, so make sure you add a little when blending fruit juices.

- Witch hazel is soothing and can be applied externally to the affected veins.

- Soak in a hot bath containing some Epsom salts twice a week.

WINTER AILMENTS

Let's face it, as the days get shorter and the skies seem to be more or less permanently grey, many people's lives seem to take on a grey mood as well. This condition is known as seasonal affective disorder or SAD for short. For some people it can be a real problem as they become irritable, anxious, lack energy and concentration, and seem prone to bouts of depression. This is not an imaginary condition, it is a result of a lack of sunlight or natural daylight during the winter months. Lack of natural light blocks the production of serotonin and stimulates the production of melatonin which is the reason you feel drowsy and sleepy for much of the time. It is trying to fool the brain into believing that it is constant night. Fortunately, there is a natural way to overcome this problem, which means that your life doesn't need to be controlled by the weather. Trick your mind into feeling happy by using artificial light. You can buy special lamps that emit 10,000 lux of white light, so make sure you sit and read for an hour in the morning under this light to fight the winter blues.

Chapter Four

Women's Ailments

Natural Remedies
for Women

The woman smiled as she stroked her girth
And said to her husband 'I'm about to give birth'.
Then her expression changed alarmingly
And she said – I might add not charmingly –
'I'm warning you now if this involves pain
You'll never use your manhood again!'

I wonder just how many women have blamed their husbands
while enduring the pain of childbirth! Too many to count I would
guess. For any men reading this book, now is the time to skip to
the next chapter as this section is purely for women.

From puberty through menstruation to the menopause, women
spend the majority of their lives juggling with hormones. Some days
we can feel on top of the world, ready to cope with anything, and
other days, particularly during times of menstruation, we want to
bury our heads under the duvet and not come out until it is all over.
This chapter is designed to help women during their journey through
life with some of the health problems they meet along the way.
Today there are shelves of products in chemists and supermarkets
specifically aimed at women. With increasing numbers of women
now turning away from prescription drugs to treat their problems,
natural products are taking a much larger role.

In granny's day menstruation was a painful hindrance without
the luxury of tampons or super-absorbent pads. Before disposable
pads came along in the 1940s, women had to use cloths or rags
which couldn't simply be thrown away. They had the embarrassment

of having to wash them and reuse them time and time again. Add to that the fact that men presumed that women couldn't function normally during a period and that it was a taboo subject not to be discussed on any account, it is no wonder that women wanted a miracle cure to an everyday problem.

Granny didn't have the luxury of choice, particularly in childbirth – none of these fancy birthing pools, epidurals, or modern pain relievers. You might think that natural childbirth is a thing of the past, but strangely that is not the case. More and more women are realizing the benefits as they become more aware of the harm that medication can do to their unborn child.

Then comes the trauma of menopause which is also known as the 'change of life', an apt name as it brings both emotional and physical changes for women. Granny wasn't offered HRT to help with the hot flushes, night sweats, and mood swings which many women suffer during this time. If you don't know what to expect it can be overwhelming as the levels of female hormones fall and your body stops producing eggs. Some women are not happy to take hormone replacements and head for natural alternatives, many of which can be a tremendous comfort to someone entering their twilight years. The best way to treat menopause is not like an illness but as the opening of a new period in your life – offering you liberation from menstruation and the end of worrying about unplanned pregnancy. Speaking from experience I have enjoyed my latter years and, apart from gravity taking over in a few places, my attitude towards life hasn't really changed an iota from when I was a young woman.

Diet and exercise can play a huge role in keeping you active and well at any time of life, which is why I keep repeating myself, repeating myself – see what I mean! If you are affected by any of the problems in this chapter give some of my remedies a go, but do remember that if you are pregnant you will need to consult a doctor before trying any alternative therapies.

Women's Problems

CYSTITIS

Cystitis is an inflammation of the bladder, something that women are more prone to than men because the female urethra is shorter and more vulnerable to infection. It is very uncomfortable, with symptoms that include urgency to urinate and the frequent passing of small amounts of urine accompanied by a burning or stinging sensation. If the condition becomes severe, then the patient may notice blood in her urine and can experience a mild fever. For many women the problem is triggered by irritation during sexual intercourse, so a piece of useful advice is to try and remember to urinate first – that is of course if you are not overcome by uncontrollable passion! If you have severe or recurrent cystitis it is advisable to consult your doctor to make sure you don't have an underlying problem.

Treatment

- Drink a glass of water containing a teaspoon of bicarbonate of soda four to five times a day.

- Drink a glass of barley water every 20 minutes or so to help reduce the stinging sensation and pain.

- Cranberry juice is one of the best natural remedies for cystitis as it prevents the growth of bacteria. Drink three glasses a day until the symptoms subside.

- Avoid tea and coffee and replace hot drinks with green tea as it contains antioxidants which will help the body fight infection.

- Make nettle tea from fresh or dried leaves, using one or two teaspoons per cup of boiling water. Drink three times a day.

- Always make sure you wash yourself from front to back.

- Try to wear undergarments that allow a bit of air to get to your parts.

- Always drink plenty of water to dilute your urine.

- Urinate as soon as you feel the urge.

- Use unscented soap and avoid all scented products in your personal region.

- Avoid drinking too much alcohol as it can aggravate cystitis.

- Include probiotic yogurt in your diet to help build up good bacteria in your system, particularly if you have had to resort to taking antibiotics.

FLUID RETENTION

Fluid retention in women is often associated with premenstrual syndrome (PMS) and pregnancy, when hormonal fluctuations can play havoc in a woman's body. When the levels of oestrogen rise it encourages the hormone aldosterone to build up, which in turn causes the kidneys to retain fluids. The areas that seem to suffer the most are the feet, ankles, and legs, but for some women no part of the body is immune and they feel like a bloated whale. If the swelling is in the legs, then keeping the legs elevated on something soft like a cushion or pillow will allow gravity to assist in draining the fluid back towards the heart. Also, regularly rotate your ankles throughout the day to help prevent the build-up of fluids. There are other home remedies to banish some of those extra fluids, so why not try some of these as well. Remember, though, although PMS can be a major cause of fluid retention, there could also be an underlying problem with the kidneys, heart, liver, or thyroid, so it is best to have a medical check-up if the condition persists.

Treatment
- Although you might think your body doesn't need any more fluids, you should drink plenty of water to make your kidneys function efficiently.

- Avoid tea, coffee, and alcohol, because these all have a dehydrating effect which can lead to fluid retention.

- Reduce your salt intake, especially around the time when you expect your period, as sodium increases fluid retention.

- Eat foods that are rich in potassium such as bananas, raisins, spinach, dried apricots, or brazil nuts.

- Add fresh parsley to your diet as it is a natural diuretic and stimulates the removal of toxins via your kidneys.

- If your ankles are swollen in hot weather, plunge your feet into a bowl of iced water, or a bag of frozen peas works well if applied to the puffy area.

MENSTRUAL PROBLEMS
Women have two major sex hormones – oestrogen and progesterone – both of which are produced in the ovaries. When a girl reaches the age of about 12 or 13, the ovaries start producing large quantities of oestrogen to help her develop into a young woman. This is generally the time when menstruation begins, signalling the reproductive stage in her life. Women can suffer different symptoms during their

menstrual cycle. Before the bleeding starts many women experience depression, headaches, painful breasts, insomnia, and a general feeling of irritability. When the menstrual flow starts, they can have cramping pains which can last for just a few hours or, for the unlucky ones, several days. Bleeding can be quite heavy or minimal and most of these problems are due to a hormonal imbalance. There are many medications available to help with menstruation problems, but there are also many natural remedies that can be very beneficial during this time.

Treatment

- One of the most effective natural remedies for menstrual problems is the regular consumption of parsley, either the raw leaves or in the form of a juice (other vegetables can be mixed with it). This is because parsley contains apiol, which is a constituent of oestrogen. Taken regularly, parsley can help with cramps and regulate the flow and regularity of your periods.

- Crush a piece of fresh ginger and boil it in a cupful of water for a few minutes. Sweeten with sugar or honey and drink after each meal.

- Eat a teaspoon of sesame seeds with a glass of hot water twice a day to reduce spasmodic cramps.

- Eating unripe papaya can help with the contractions of the muscles that cause cramp during menstruation.

- Chamomile tea can be very soothing and help relax the muscles that are causing the cramp.

- If you are a smoker, then try to give up during the days just before and during your period, as smoke can aggravate menstrual disorders.

● Remember, even though you probably won't feel like it, exercise is beneficial during this time, as it will help speed up the bleeding and will possibly shorten the length of the period.

● For excessive bleeding, boil one teaspoon of coriander seeds in two cupfuls of water and reduce until it is half the quanity. Add sugar to taste and drink while still warm, twice or three times a day.

THRUSH

Thrush is the common name for a fungal infection of the mucous membranes by the yeast *Candida albicans*. It is most commonly a vaginal infection and often occurs in pregnant women due to the changes in their hormones which can cause bacteria. The symptoms include itching and irritation and sometimes a burning sensation. Thrush will not cause any problems to an unborn baby, but it can be passed on to your baby as it emerges from the birth canal or to your partner during intercourse, so it must never go untreated. People often experience thrush after a course of antibiotics which destroy the helpful bacteria in our bodies. There are several things that women can do to try and avoid thrush, so take heed as prevention is better than cure.

Treatment

● Include live natural yogurt in your diet on a daily basis to build up your immunity and, if thrush rears its ugly head, apply it topically to the vaginal area.

● Use garlic regularly in your cooking as it has been found to be effective in dealing with vaginal infections.

- Use one or two drops of tea tree oil in your bath and soak for about 15 minutes. If you experience any skin irritation as a result of the oil, stop using it immediately.

- Try to avoid any clothes that do not allow air to circulate, like nylon tights or tight-fitting jeans. Wear natural cotton next to your skin rather than synthetic fibres.

- Avoid using perfumed soap or shower gels in your personal region and change to non-biological washing powder for your laundry.

- After you have used the toilet make sure you wipe from front to back to avoid contamination with bacteria.

- Never use a flannel to wash this area as it may harbour germs.

- Do not use vaginal deodorants and make sure you dry yourself properly after swimming or bathing.

Pregnancy and Childbirth

Although a distant memory for me, I remember in the last few weeks of my pregnancy a feeling of apprehension and excitement as the time got closer to the impending birth. It is quite normal to feel nervous about labour and childbirth, especially if it is your first baby. After all, it is like stepping into the unknown, no matter how many books you read on the subject. Years ago before the advent of modern hospitals, equipment, and drugs, midwives would prepare herbs – old remedies that had been handed down from generation to generation – to assist the mother in her journey ahead. Many of these old customs have been lost over the centuries, but today many women are opting for a completely natural birth as they believe it is so much better for their unborn child. Although we can rest easy that modern technology can take over if things should go wrong, there is no harm in asking if you can try to give birth the natural way. That means trying to have the baby without the assistance of conventional medications. My daughter decided to take this route and managed exceedingly well by using a TENS machine (Transcutaneous Electrical Nerve Stimulator) to control the pain. These work by delivering small electrical pulses to the body via electrodes placed on the skin. With the right preparation and support, women can experience natural childbirth without having to endure too much stress or discomfort. Remember, though, you should never feel guilty if you find it all too much and have to resort to more modern methods of relieving the pain. If you should decide to try some of the more natural remedies to ease pain, discuss the matter with your doctor or midwife first to make sure you are not doing more harm than good.

HELP WITH LABOUR PAINS

The amount of pain experienced by women during childbirth varies greatly, and will depend on the woman's natural pain threshold and her state of mind. Those of you who are opting for a natural birth might like to consider trying some of these methods to help you deal with the pain associated with the various stages of labour.

- As soon as you feel the first signs of labour, try to eat something light. This won't help with the pain but it might be a long time before you get something to eat as the hospital or birthing centre may discourage it.

- Make sure you drink plenty of liquids, as dehydration can make your contractions more painful. Try having a sip of water or fruit juice after each contraction.

- Make sure you urinate regularly as a full bladder can add to labour pain.

- Try sitting, lying or standing in different positions to find out which is the most comfortable for you. I always found sitting on my legs and bouncing up and down during a contraction worked wonders.

- Get your birthing partner to put a hot compress on your lower abdomen just above the pubic bone, either between or during contractions.

- If you have access to one, step into a hot shower. Many women find the warmth of the water provides comfort and relaxation.

- Most important, remember to 'breathe'. This is when all the hours of practice come in handy. If you are not able to relax your muscles properly, the baby will have problems in descending. Deep breathing can help to keep your levels of anxiety down.

- Some women like to have their backs massaged, while others can't stand to be touched during labour – that one is up to you.

MORNING SICKNESS

It is estimated that at least half of all pregnant women experience some nausea or vomiting during the first 12 weeks or so of their pregnancy. Although called 'morning' sickness, it can actually occur at any time of the day and can really spoil the excitement about being pregnant. If you are one of the unlucky ones, then hopefully some of these suggestions might get you through those first difficult months.

Treatment

● Make sure you eat small amounts frequently so that your stomach is never empty or too full as you do not want your blood sugar levels to drop drastically.

● Avoid fatty or fried foods.

● Nibble on some crystallized ginger.

● Keep some dry crackers or biscuits by your bed and make sure you eat a couple before getting out of bed. Or you could ask your hubby to make you a nice piece of toast.

● Drink mint or chamomile tea to help settle the stomach.

● Eating a piece of fruit when hungry can help keep nausea at bay.

PROBLEMS ASSOCIATED WITH BREASTFEEDING

Most new mothers look forward to the moment they can put their baby to their breast, hoping to encourage a rapid bonding. There is no doubt that breast milk is the best food for a newborn, and there is nothing that even comes close to it for providing the nutrients and protection the baby will need in later life. Sometimes a new mother can find breastfeeding a bit of a challenge, especially if her nipples become sore, her breasts become engorged, or she experiences a nasty bout of mastitis. In an effort to try and make the problems associated with breastfeeding less daunting, try a few of these natural remedies that granny used to swear by.

Treatment for engorged breasts

- If your breasts become engorged, which is very common in the first two or three weeks after delivery, try taking a handful of comfrey leaves, wrap them in a piece of muslin and steam them for a few minutes. Place the warm muslin on your breast to help ease the pressure.

- Soak a towel in hot water, ring it out, and place it on the breast for about ten minutes before feeding.

- Try feeding your baby frequently on both breasts for periods of 10 to 15 minutes.

Treatment for mastitis

Mastitis is a painful condition that results from bacteria entering the breast via a tiny crack on the nipple. Make sure you seek medical advice if the condition becomes serious.

- Place hot towels on the breast or run hot water over them in the shower to help ease the pain.

- Drink plenty of water and make sure you get plenty of rest.

- Continue to nurse the baby as often and as long as required as the breast infection will not make the infant sick.

- Take two to three drops of bee propolis (a resinous substance bees collect from tree buds) as a tincture twice a day.

- Take a tincture of echinacea root for at least a week until the symptoms have cleared. Use one drop for every 2 lb (0.9 kg) of body weight.

Cracked nipples

- Use calendula cream to soothe the pain of cracked nipples as it is safe for the baby to swallow.

- To prevent cracked nipples, rub them with a mixture of pure lemon juice and olive oil throughout pregnancy.

- Honey, mixed with either olive oil or lanolin, has a softening and moisturizing effect on cracked nipples. Make sure you are not allergic to lanolin before using it and wash off before feeding.

- Take extra precautions such as washing your nipples in plain water after feeds and keeping them dry with breast pads.

- Do not clean nipples with soap as this can lead to cracking.

- Expose the nipples to air for some time every day.

Low milk supply

There are a number of factors that can influence the amount of milk you produce, but it is usually down to how often you put your baby to your breast and how well the breast is emptied at each feed. Suckling stimulates the hormone (prolactin) that produces milk, so the more often the baby feeds, the more your milk will increase. People have suggested to me that they take various herbal concoctions to help increase the milk flow, but quite honestly I think if you just adhere to a few simple rules, nine out of ten times the problem solves itself. Try breastfeeding your baby on demand, the more feeds the better. Feed for longer and make sure one breast is empty before moving to the next. It is very important that you get enough rest and drink plenty of fluids. Avoid smoking and excessive intake of caffeine. If you still have a problem talk to your friendly midwife or doctor.

Chapter Five

Children's Ailments

Natural Remedies for Children

Childhood is about a scraped knee
Or being stung by a bumble bee
Childhood is wearing itchy clothes
And having to wear silly bows
Childhood is giving granny a hug
Cos she found a cure for your nasty bug.

There isn't anything as heart-wrenching as seeing a young child in pain or lying in bed trying to fight off a fever. As a mother and a granny there have been many occasions when I would gladly have taken their place, so if I could come up with a quick-acting remedy so much the better. If we can find ways of boosting their immune system to help them fight off colds and other illnesses, or find a soothing cream to stop the graze on their knee becoming infected, then we are helping their bodies repair themselves naturally.

Because children have a much faster metabolism than us, they often show signs of illness by running a temperature. It is their little bodies' way of trying to rid the system of the foreign toxins. It is not necessary to run to the doctor every time your child has a sore throat, an earache, or a nasty pain in the tummy – granny usually has the answer with some of her old-fashioned remedies. Of course if the symptoms are severe, it goes without saying that you should call a doctor straight away. Natural treatments rarely have side effects, cost you next to nothing, and use products that you probably already have in the house or garden. I know my granny always gave me a hot drink of lemon and honey as soon as I felt a sore throat coming on.

COLIC

Any parent who has had the experience of a colicky baby will know just how stressful and exhausting it can be. Colic in babies and infants is normally a sign of trapped wind and is generally more common in bottle-fed babies. The baby's body language will soon alert you to the fact that it is uncomfortable. They usually go red in the face and pull their legs up in an attempt to relieve the pain in their stomach. In my day you headed straight for the bottle of gripe water which usually had the desired effect. My daughter – a much more modern mum – won't touch the proprietary brands of gripe water because, in her words, they contained a lot of unnecessary 'rubbish'. I decided to search granny's dog-eared archives that I mentioned earlier, and lo and behold she had scribbled out a recipe to cure what she referred to as the 'baby gripes' – see the recipe on page 124.

Ways of helping colic

- Make sure you always burp the baby properly during and after feeding.

- You might find it helps to lay the baby across your lap on its tummy and give it a warming rub on the back.

- Try to avoid eating spicy or very rich food while you are breast-feeding.

- A warm bath can be soothing to the baby and help provide some relief from the discomfort. This is one of the simplest and best cures for settling a colicky baby.

- Motion will often help a baby with colic and some parents resort to pushing them around in the pram until they settle.

Granny's Cure for Baby Gripes

You will need
1 teaspoon fennel or dill seeds, crushed
1 pint boiled water

Method
1. Pour the boiled water over the crushed fennel or dill seeds and allow to steep for about 20 minutes.
2. Strain through fine muslin and discard the seeds.
3. Store in the refrigerator and use when needed.

This gripe water should be discarded after 24 hours as it starts to lose its potency. If you do purchase gripe water make sure it does not contain any alcohol, sodium bicarbonate, artificial colouring, or any other non-natural products.

CRADLE CAP

Cradle cap is really an infant form of dandruff and is caused by the baby's oil glands being overproductive. It is a very common condition and even though it looks uncomfortable, it doesn't cause the baby any discomfort. Some new mothers worry that they are doing something wrong, but that is not the case. Once the baby's sebaceous glands settle into a routine, the cradle cap should disappear naturally. If you want to give it a helping hand try one of the following.

- Rub some almond or olive oil into your baby's scalp, leave for an hour, and then wash off using a mild baby shampoo.

- Add two drops of tea tree oil to olive oil and massage into the scalp before bathing.

EARACHE

Earache is a troublesome condition which occurs more frequently in children than adults. Earache can be caused by any number of things such as an infection in the middle ear, excessive earwax, a perforated eardrum, or a problem associated with the ear, nose or throat following or during a cold. Earaches can occur quite suddenly, but are often difficult to diagnose in a young child as they are unable to tell you what is wrong. If you see a child constantly tugging at its ears and they don't seem their usual bright self, then the chances are they have an earache. Before taking any action get a torch and check inside the ears to make sure they haven't got some small toy stuck in there!

Treatment

● Take a teaspoon of sesame oil and add half a clove of garlic. Warm the oil, then lie the child on its side on a bed. Put four drops of oil in the ear and get the child to lie there for as long as possible, then turn them over and do the same on the other side.

● Other oils you can use are warmed mustard oil, or olive oil with a few drops of tea tree oil added to it.

● Garlic is a natural antibiotic, so extract the juice of a few cloves and put a few drops into each ear.

● Apply some heat to the aching ear using a heating pad or a warm cloth.

● Remember to keep your child's ears covered during cold or very windy weather.

● If you are taking your child on an aeroplane, make sure the child has something to chew when taking off or landing.

FEVER

Fever is still one of the most common concerns for parents and will often send them running to the emergency department of their local hospital. Fever itself is not life-threatening unless it is persistently high, and it is usually caused by a common infection. It is the body's way of trying to fight off the infection on its own. If your child is showing any of these signs – being fussy, irritable, lethargic, quiet, feels warm to the touch, is not eating, and keeps crying – then it is worth taking their temperature. Your child is showing signs of fever if their temperature is as follows:

Rectal temperature (anus) is at or higher than 38°C (100.4°F).
Oral temperature (mouth) is at or higher than 37.5°C (99.5°F).
Axilliary temperature (armpit) is at or higher than 37.2°C (99°F).

If you have serious concerns about your child, particularly if under six months of age, then you should call your doctor immediately or take them to the emergency department to be on the safe side. If you are self-treating the child at home for a mild fever, remember never give young children aspirin. There are proprietary medicines for babies and young children which you can safely use to help reduce the fever, so on this occasion I would suggest you use one of these.

Try giving your child a lukewarm sponge bath for about 15 minutes. As the water evaporates it starts to cool the body, which will help to bring down the fever. Don't use cold water as that will cause the child to shiver, and shivering will actually cause the body temperature to rise. The only other thing to do is to make sure that the child has plenty of fluids to avoid the further problem of dehydration. Keep the child as quiet as possible and remember, if the fever is not too high then it is actually working for, not against, the body to fight off infection and rid it of any toxins.

HYPERACTIVITY

Children naturally seem to have boundless energy so it can be difficult to spot the first signs of hyperactivity. Recent studies have shown that hyperactivity can be triggered by artificial colourings and preservatives that are present in certain types of food. So it may well be worth considering changing your child's diet if they are showing any signs of excessive behaviour.

● Chocolate can be a contributory factor, so think about substituting it with carob; see granny's recipe for healthy cookies on page 128. Corn or rice can be substituted for wheat, which can also add to hyperactivity. Make sure your child has a healthy diet with natural ingredients and plenty of raw fruit and vegetables, as this can have a calming effect and help to improve their concentration.

● Regular exercise, such as walking, will help provide release for hyperactivity. It provides the opportunity to release all that pent-up energy, so you might like to think about putting a trampoline in the garden.

● Music therapy can also be beneficial to hyperactive children, as the frequencies of sound help to calm the brain. So find out if there is a class near you.

If you suspect your child has problems as a result of psychological disturbances, a brain disorder, or some form of social pressure, then this problem needs careful assessment and qualified help. It is not necessarily the case that your child will be prescribed drugs that produce nasty side effects, as more and more practitioners are turning towards natural herbal remedies to treat such cases. Look at all the possibilities before deciding which route you want to take.

Granny's Carob Crunchies

You will need
240 g (8½ oz) wholewheat flour
1 tablespoon baking powder
½ teaspoon cinnamon
250 g (9 oz) chunky peanut butter
235 ml (8 fl oz) milk
200 g (7 oz) carob chips

Method
1. Preheat the oven to 200°C/400°F/gas mark 6.
2. In a large bowl, combine the flour, baking powder, and cinnamon.
3. Microwave the peanut butter for 5 to 10 seconds to soften. Whisk in the milk, then stir the mixture into the dry ingredients.
4. Work the dough with your hands and shape it into a flattened log and slice into 2.5-cm (1-in) thick pieces and spread over a baking tray. Bake until they are golden and crisp, about 15 to 20 minutes.
5. Melt the carob in a microwave or over water on the stove top. Using a spoon, drizzle the carob over the top of the biscuits and leave them to cool completely.
6. Store in an airtight container, but I can guarantee they won't be around for long.

SLEEPLESSNESS

Just like adults, children can suffer from sleeplessness due to over-stimulation or worry. The pain of teething can be another thing that might keep your child awake. Children need a regular routine and this is particularly important at bedtime. Caffeine is very often the culprit of sleeplessness in children, so make sure you read the labels carefully before giving your child any flavoured drinks. Try to eliminate chocolate from their diet, or anything chocolate-flavoured, particularly late in the day.

Tips for peaceful nights

● Give your child a nice warm bath just before bed as this helps to make them relax.

● Make bedtime a pleasant experience; try reading them a nice story before you finally tuck them in. Put a few drops of lavender oil under their pillow as this will have a calming effect.

● If you know your child is crying for attention and not because it is ill or uncomfortable, try not to comfort it immediately. Try to leave the child to stop crying on its own – it is up to you just how long you are prepared to wait.

● Never use bed as a punishment, otherwise the child will associate bedtime with a bad experience.

● If your child is easily distracted by noise, then think about playing some relaxing music in its room until it has gone to sleep.

● Give your child some warm milk before bed. This is something that has been done for generations because it works. Milk contains calcium that actually helps you sleep.

TEETHING

Babies seem to teethe at all different stages; some start at about two months while others don't even begin until they are several months old. The process of cutting baby teeth can be painful for both the baby and the parents, as it can make a baby very fretful and demand a lot of TLC. Teething is, of course, just a part of the baby's development, so if there is something in your kitchen that will ease your child's discomfort, the whole process will be a lot less stressful.

Tips for teething problems

- Put a banana in the freezer and then allow the baby to put the sweet treat to its gums.

- Put some water in a baby bottle and freeze it upside down so the water is frozen in the teat. Give it to the baby to chew when it needs a bit of teething comfort.

- If you see your baby gnawing at its fists, give it a hard, unsweetened cracker-like biscuit to gnaw on instead.

- For older children, keep some apple slices in the fridge and allow them to chew on these.

- For younger babies you can gently massage the gums with a clean, cold finger.

- Again for older children, the best thing to do is to distract them from the pain in their mouth. Do some dancing around to their favourite music – this one always works with my grandson.

Chapter Six

Fighting the Ageing Process

Ironing out the Wrinkles

Granny was always solid as a rock
You could always count on her to darn your sock
She'd always pamper to your whims
And loved to babysit the twins
But now she's taken to wearing leather
And riding her Harley whatever the weather!

Reaching the more mature years was something I wasn't really looking forward to with relish, but somehow they have crept up on me without even giving me time to prepare. I look in the mirror and the reflection that looks back at me is someone I don't know. The mind plays tricks and tells you that you are still a young woman the body, however, is not so kind. Gravity simply takes over and your once pert bits are now trying desperately to reach terra firma. When I am out with my children – who are parents themselves – I find that I am reverting to my thirties and I become one of them. Probably a major embarrassment, but luckily they say they love me as I am – nutty as a fruitcake!

Wear and tear has taken its toll and I don't spring over the stiles like I used to when out walking the dogs. I don't jump out of bed each morning, I gingerly put one leg on the floor and hope the other one will follow without too much fuss. I can still touch my toes – just – but the rush of blood to my head makes me feel quite lightheaded for a couple of minutes afterwards, so I try to avoid it if I can.

I like to think I take care of myself – I eat well, I exercise, and don't overindulge in anything I shouldn't any more. My system has never been able to tolerate medicines, so if there was a natural alternative

I have always headed down that route. For the aches and pains, the wrinkles, and any other ailment that is associated with this thing they call 'old age', read on.

ARTHRITIS

The word 'arthritis' quite literally means 'inflammation of the joints' and although there are different strains of the disease, the two most common forms are osteoarthritis, which develops from general wear and tear of the joints, and rheumatoid arthritis, which is a different problem altogether. It is a serious condition in which the body's own defences, for some unknown reason, start to attack its own cells. Osteoarthritis sufferers experience stiffness and pain in the joints, but with rheumatoid arthritis the whole body can be affected and it can even lead to deformity in the hands and feet. Anyone suffering from the latter will need to seek professional advice as there can be underlying problems associated with this disease.

Treatment

- One age-old natural remedy for arthritis is the use of raw potato juice which is considered to be one of the most successful biological treatments for conditions related to the joints. You can either slice up a medium-sized potato with its skin still on and leave it soaking in a bowl full of clean water overnight, or you can use a juicer and extract all the juice which should then be diluted with water. Either of these should be drunk first thing in the morning on an empty stomach.

- The alkaline action of raw vegetable juices helps to dissolve the accumulation of deposits around the joints. So drink a glass of green leafy vegetable juice mixed in equal proportions with carrot, celery, and beetroot each day.

- Either eating fresh pineapple or drinking it as a juice is beneficial to arthritis as it contains the enzyme bromelin which helps to reduce swelling and inflammation in the joints.

- Soak some sesame seeds in a quarter-cup of water overnight. Drink the water in which the seeds were soaked first thing in the morning.

- Wearing a copper bracelet can help strengthen the muscular system. Alternatively, store water overnight in a copper container and drink first thing in the morning.

- Garlic is another effective remedy for arthritis as it contains an anti-inflammatory property. It can either be taken raw or as an ingredient in your cooking.

- Bananas are a rich source of vitamin B6, which is useful in the treatment of arthritis.

- The citric acid in lime juice is also beneficial and should be taken once a day, preferably first thing in the morning, diluted in water.

- Red pepper has a pain-relieving chemical which triggers the body to release endorphins, nature's own opiates.

- Massage sore joints with a warm coconut or mustard oil mixed with two or three pieces of camphor.

- Steam the fresh leaves of a stinging nettle and eat them as a vegetable. You will be pleased to know that the fuzzy stingers lose their sting when the leaves are cooked.

GOUT

Gout is a form of athritis because it causes pains in the joints. It is caused by a build-up of uric acid crystals in the joints, skin and kidneys and seems mainly to affect the joint of the big toe, causing swelling and a great deal of pain. It has been associated with drinking alcohol to excess, lack of exercise, and rich foods which is why it was called 'rich man's disease' 300 years ago. It chiefly affects men over the age of 30, but some women are affected by the disease after the menopause. It is a serious condition which will need medical intervention, but anyone who suffers from this disease might like to try some of the more natural approaches to help relieve the pain.

Treatment

Follow all the same treatments as for arthritis, but also try:

- Fresh cherries are believed to be beneficial for gout. To start with the patient should eat about 15 to 20 cherries a day, but as the disease comes under control this can be reduced to ten.

- The malic acid found in apples helps to neutralize the uric acid and can afford relief to gout sufferers. Eat one apple after each meal.

- Eat plenty of avocado as it helps to lower uric acid levels in the blood.

- Bathe the feet in a warm soak containing about 500 grams (1 lb) of Epsom salts.

- Bananas are thought to be beneficial in the treatment of gout, so include one a day in your diet.

MENOPAUSE

Here I am again, back on my favourite subject – the change of life. It is the time in a woman's life when her periods cease or become more erratic and her reproductive system closes down. No two women will experience the same symptoms during this phase of their life, and it is up to the individual as to whether they want to take a course of hormone replacement therapy or rely on the old and trusted methods. Some women sail through the menopause without any unpleasant symptoms. Unfortunately, however, there are many women who develop any or all of the following – hot flushes, night sweats, insomnia, tension, low libido, irritability, depression, fatigue, headaches, palpitations – all due to an imbalance of hormones.

Treatment

- Follow a healthy exercise routine as this will help your bones and muscles, and with keeping your heart healthy.

- Eat foods rich in calcium as the lack of ovarian hormones can result in severe calcium deficiency. Any woman experiencing disturbing symptoms might like to consider taking a supplement as well, but remember, milk, cheese, yogurt, and cream should be a permanent part of your diet at this time.

- Drink 60 to 90 ml (4 to 6 tbsp) of beetreet juice, two to three times a day.

- Liquorice contains natural oestrogenic compounds which can help when your levels of oestrogen are too low. The recommended quantity is about 5 grams (0.12 oz) per day.

- Eat foods rich in boron which can help to increase the blood levels of circulating oestrogen. These foods include apples, apricots, asparagus, beetroot, broccoli, cabbage, cherries, currants, dill and cumin seeds, dandelion, figs, peaches, parsley, pears, poppy seeds, strawberries, and tomatoes.

● Other foods that contain phytoestrogens are apples, celery, dates, fennel, and pomegranates and these should be included regularly in your diet.

● Magnesium is a very important mineral for your bones and general well-being, as it is known as 'nature's tranquillizer'. It will help with symptoms such as anxiety, irritability, and other mood changes so eat plenty of the following foods – black beans, raw broccoli, halibut, peanuts, okra, oysters, raw plantain, scallops, pumpkin and squash seeds, soya milk, spinach, tofu, and wholegrain cereals and bread.

OSTEOPOROSIS

Osteoporosis is a disease caused by the loss of calcium which weakens the bones and leaves them brittle. It is one of the most common conditions associated with ageing and affects many more women than men. Thin, petite women are more at risk so they need to make sure their diet is good and that they keep up a regular form of exercise. Protein can leach calcium from the bones, so try to keep your protein to the bare minimum. Possible symptoms of osteoporosis include lower back pain, loss of height (can be up to several inches), stooped posture, and increased risk of fractures, particularly of the hip.

Treatment

● Amazingly, black pepper (*Piper nigrum*) contains four anti-osteoporosis compounds, so sprinkle generously on, say, your avocado or salad, as every little bit helps.

- Parsley is one of the highest food sources to strengthen bones, as it contains fluorine, so don't throw away that garnish – eat it!

- Dandelions and cabbage are rich in boron, so make sure you include these in your diet.

- Avocado is a good source of vitamins D and E and can help the body turn calcium into bone. Mash some avocado into some low-fat cottage cheese and you can get a good dose of calcium at the same time.

- Soya beans are very rich in phytoestrogens so can help when oestrogen levels are low.

POOR CIRCULATION

Poor circulation to the extremities is quite common in elderly people, or those who do little exercise. It can lead to more serious problems such as phlebitis or thrombosis, so it should not be neglected. Seek professional medical help if you are in any doubt.

Tips to prevent, treat, and improve circulation

- Exercise is by far the best way to keep your blood flowing round your body. Try walking, swimming, or a gentle bike ride to get your heart pumping.

- Eat a well-balanced diet that is high in fibre and low in fat; this will keep your cholesterol levels in check.

- Take supplements such as cod liver oil and omega 3 fish oils.

- If you are a smoker, now is the time to quit. It is no good saying 'I am too old to worry about it now!', the truth is it is never too late.

Smoking can harden the arteries which causes other blood vessels to constrict.

● Wear support socks or hosiery to improve poor circulation.

● Taking a warm bath, or soaking your feet in warm water, will help to increase the flow of blood to your extremities.

● Make sure you keep your hands and feet warm in the winter months by wearing thermal or woollen socks and gloves.

● Try to keep your stress levels to a minimum. Yoga, deep breathing exercises, and soothing music should help to calm you down.

● If your feet are swollen, raise them up by resting them on a pillow to allow any fluid to drain from the feet.

● Remember, if you sit around for too long you risk getting poor circulation, so make sure you keep getting up and moving around.

● Eat plenty of garlic; not only is it a great additive for cooking, it is also good at improving the circulation. It helps to lower blood pressure and keeps arteries strong and clear as well.

● Cayenne pepper is one of the strongest circulatory stimulants, so use plenty in cooking and sprinkle it on your food as well.

WRINKLES

Wrinkles come to us all, whether we like it or not. With age the skin starts to lose its elasticity and moisture and wrinkles start to appear, particularly around the eyes, mouth, and neck. Too much exposure to the sun is one of the main reasons for premature ageing of the skin, so make sure you use plenty of sunscreen if you like spending a lot of time outdoors. You can spend a fortune on fancy creams and lotions claiming to work miracles and, being the old cynic that I am, I believe many of the manufacturer's claims are a load of old bunkum. Try some of my more natural remedies to help keep the skin supple and youthful; at least I know these work.

Ward off wrinkles

- Eat at least two raw carrots each day as they are high in vitamin A which helps alleviate dry skin and wrinkling.

- Cucumbers are cheaper and probably just as effective as commercial moisturizers. Cut them into disk-shaped pieces and rub them on your skin.

- Combine honey, olive oil, and a fragrance-free moisturizer and use daily to keep your skin supple.

- Apply lemon juice to any unsightly age spots as this will help them to fade gradually.

- Drink chamomile tea made from two teaspoons of crushed dried leaves per cup of boiling water.

- Eating some shredded ginger with honey will help give your skin a healthy glow.

- Gently massage almond oil into the skin to keep wrinkles at bay.

- To help remove dead skin cells, crush some grapes and apply the mash as a facial mask. Rinse it off after 15 to 30 minutes.

Chapter Seven

Aaaagh!

The Nervous
System

Soothe that Stress

Your fists are clenched, your jaw is tight
You are tired and ready for a fight
Stop! the best medicine is laughter
It will keep you happy hereafter
So wake up, smile, and say
Life is great – stress – no way!

Remember it is quite normal to feel anxious from time to time, that is just a part of everyday life. I remember vividly the day I had to take my 11-plus examination and being awake for most of the night worrying about it. I remember mother coming into my room after seeing the light shining underneath my door, and handing me a stick of liquorice. I thought it was just a treat to make me feel better, but now I know that it has many ingredients that combat stress and depression. All the anxiety left me tired and crotchety, but I survived and passed the exam with flying colours.

If symptoms of anxiety and depression constantly plague you and you feel you are not getting the quality of life you deserve, don't just put up with it, try some of granny's remedies before rushing off to the doctor for an antidepressant. Of course, if your symptoms are really debilitating, then the doctor is the only course of action to take. My son always says that his little 'worry worm' is like his friend, as it keeps him on his toes at work and means he gets a lot more done. This is when you use stress to your advantage and don't let it get on top of you. One of the worst side effects of anxiety and stress is insomnia, so if we can find ways of learning to relax and turning our minds off when we go to bed, it gives us the energy to get through the next day without feeling the whole world is resting on our shoulders.

ANXIETY

Anxiety can leave people feeling restless, tense or on edge, irritable, impatient, and with a low level of concentration. They may also notice changes in their physical health, such as headaches, jaw pain, muscle tension, difficulty falling or staying asleep, dry mouth, general fatigue, a tightness in the chest, indigestion, bloating, and excessive sweating. Anxiety can become a major problem when a person starts to dread facing the day ahead and even the smallest of tasks can become a major hurdle. This type of anxiety is never a good thing as your immune system will not be strong enough to fight off germs and viruses, so make sure you do something about it. For centuries, tea including chamomile, cloves, lavender, and thyme, has been used to treat a variety of stress-related illnesses.

Coping with anxiety

● St John's Wort is probably the most common herb used in treating anxiety as it has an active compound called hypericin. It can help with sleep disorders and calm jangling nerves, but you should seek medical advice before embarking on self-medication.

● Staying active is a great way to combat symptoms of anxiety, as a rush of adrenaline can bring back that 'feel good' factor.

● Many people are able to calm themselves down by using deep breathing techniques.

● Ginger is also good at lifting spirits, so chew on a few pieces of crystallized ginger, or drink some ginger and honey tea.

● Avoid anything that contains caffeine, as it can exacerbate feelings of anxiety and remember this is not just coffee and tea, chocolate contains caffeine, too.

- Take a warm cup of chamomile tea up to the bathroom and soak in a lovely hot bath that contains some lavender oil. To really spoil yourself, listen to some of your favourite music and your anxious thoughts will dissolve in the steam.

- Eat foods that are rich in vitamin B, as they contain neuro-transmitters which allow the nerve cells to function as they should. Whole grains, such as wheat and oats, fish and seafood, poultry and meat, eggs, dairy products, leafy green vegetables, beans, and peas should all be a regular part of your daily diet.

- Finally, if you really feel that things are getting on top of you, pick up the phone and speak to a close friend, especially if they are good at making you laugh. This will soon lift your mood.

DEPRESSION

The following remedies are only for people who suffer from mild bouts of depression; anyone who has deep or continuing instances of depression must seek professional help. It is normal to feel depressed if something bad has happened in your life, but if there is no logical reason behind the 'blues' then you are probably suffering from clinical depression which will need medical help. So if you are somone who has the blues from time to time, try one of the following remedies to lift your spirits.

Treating the blues

- Try all the remedies listed under Anxiety on page 143 and this page, or any of those listed below.

- Cashew nuts are rich in vitamin B, thiamine, and riboflavin, all of which can stimulate the appetite and help to get the happy feeling back.

- Apples are a valuable remedy in dealing with depression. Apples contain vitamin B, phosphorus, and potassium which help produce glutamic acid which, in turn, controls the wear and tear of the nerve cells. Eat at least one apple each day with a glass of milk containing a little honey.

- Cardamom has proved valuable in treating depression. Crush some seeds and steep in boiling water to make a tea with a very pleasant aroma.

- The root of asparagus is good for the brain and nerves. Try and get hold of some powdered root and take one to two grams daily.

- Make an infusion of rose petals by mixing 15 grams (1 teaspoon) of petals to 250 ml (9 fl oz) of boiling water. Drink a glass occasionally to help lift those blue moments.

INSOMNIA

Insomnia is a general term that applies to the inability to fall asleep or stay asleep for any length of time. People generally need less sleep as they get older, so don't be surprised if granny is up at six in the morning and then has a little doze after lunch. Some people become obsessed with trying to get at least eight hours' sleep a night. This is not always necessary as it is the quality of sleep not the quantity that counts. The most common cause of insomnia is mental anxiety which is brought about by overwork, overexcitement, or just worrying about something that you are not looking forward to. This is quite normal and should adjust itself as soon as the period of anxiety passes. Try to take your mind off whatever is bothering you and use the old favourite of counting sheep – see how many you can get up to before drifting off. If, however, insomnia is a nightly occurrence for no apparent reason it can cause loss of coordination, confusion, and bouts of depression, so you should seek medical help. Sleeping pills have become big business, something which granny couldn't turn to, so why not try some of the more natural ways of inducing sleep.

Treating sleeplessness

- Eat a diet rich in thiamine or vitamin B, so make sure you include plenty of wholegrain cereals, pulses, and nuts.

- Lettuce is good at inducing sleep as it contains lectucarium. The juice of lettuce can have a mild sedative effect which will help you drift off to sleep.

- Drink a glass of milk sweetened with honey just before you go to bed as it acts as a tonic and a tranquillizer.

- Make a tea from aniseed (one teaspoon) and 375 ml of boiling water. Allow it to infuse for 15 minutes, strain and drink while still warm. Drink after meals or just before going to bed.

- Honey has a hypnotic effect which induces sound sleep. It should be taken with water just before going to bed. Use two teaspoons to a cup of water. This is also safe to give to babies over a year old.

- Avoid any food that includes caffeine and try to stick to a low salt diet, as these are both said to interfere with sleep.

- Make sure you take regular exercise during the day. Or enrol in your local yoga class as this can provide mental relaxation and eliminate those nighttime worries.

- Avoid taking naps during the day.

NEURALGIA

Neuralgia is a disorder that results in severe, spasmodic pain along one or more nerves. The pain is usually sharp and shooting and, in severe cases, can be quite debilitating. It seems to affect the older generation and, unfortunately, it cannot be cured by regular analgesics, so a simple home remedy to stop the pain would be a great relief for many people. It can be triggered by stress, migraines, dental problems, or shingles, but don't despair, there is a very simple cure out there and that is *celery*. My blacksmith, who was only 44 years old at the time, was suffering from shingles and couldn't work because he was in so much pain. I told him about drinking celery juice and that it really works. He tried it and he said within one hour the pain had subsided considerably. He drank a glass every day until the symptoms had cleared up and, hey presto, no more neuralgia!

SCIATICA

Sciatica is a condition that involves pain that runs from the lower back to the buttocks and/or the outer back of the leg. It is caused by pressure on the sciatic nerve following damage to a disc in the back. Natural remedies for sciatica are not only cheap but easy to take, but like most illnesses you should consult a doctor before embarking on any natural cure remedies.

Treating sciatica

● Drink a combination of potato juice and celery leaves on a regular basis to obtain relief from the pain of sciatica. You can add extra benefit by including the juice of carrots and beetroot.

● Drink plenty of pure celery juice to relieve the pain.

● Garlic is another good natural cure for sciatica pain. Either eat raw or use several cloves in your favourite recipes.

Granny's Mustard Plaster

Mustard plasters have been used as a home treatment for respiratory disorders and sciatica for centuries. Mustard has a soothing effect by warming the skin, while its counter-irritant properties cause a mild irritation, which distracts the body from the deeper pain of sciatica.

You will need
½ teaspoon mustard powder
1 tablespoon plain flour
water

Method
1. Tear a piece of fabric from an old, clean shirt, sheet, or pair of pyjamas about 30 x 15 cm (12 x 6 in).
2. Mix half a teaspoon of mustard seed powder with one tablespoon of flour.
3. Add cool water to the mixture until it resembles a fairly thick paste.
4. Spread the paste on half of the piece of fabric and then fold over the other half to make a sandwich.
5. Place on a plate and warm in a low oven or microwave, but make sure it doesn't get too hot, otherwise the flour will cook and become solid.
6. Place the mustard plaster on the sore area and attach using an elastic bandage.

Warning: You will need to check the skin every couple of hours to make sure it is not too sensitive and burning. If you wish to leave it on overnight, reduce the amount of mustard in the plaster, so that the skin will not overreact.

- Massage the affected area using some warmed garlic oil.

- Make a poultice out of stinging nettle leaves and apply it to the painful area. Make sure you wear gloves whenever you handle this plant to protect yourself from its stingers.

SHINGLES

Shingles is chicken pox that has come back to haunt you in older life. It is caused by the herpes virus, which lies dormant in the nerve cells following the childhood illness. The symptoms include an extremely painful rash that usually appears on the face and torso, which develops into chicken pox-type blisters that finally crust over and generally heal in about two to three weeks. Some people who suffer from shingles say the excruciating pain lasts for many months, sometimes years, and this is called postherpetic neuralgia. Make sure you see your doctor if you suspect you are suffering from shingles.

Helping shingles sufferers
- As explained in the section on Neuralgia on page 147, celery juice can be beneficial to treat the pain associated with this disease.

- Try mixing a mint tea with lots of lemon balm, as both are good at working against the herpes virus.

- A gel made from liquorice root appears to be an excellent topical application. Rub it on the affected areas and you will find that any serious pain and inflammation should clear up after about three days.

- Pear juice is rich in antiviral caffeic acid, which is a natural antioxidant. It works by targeting the virus that causes shingles. Drink fresh pear juice or eat lots of pears for rapid relief.

● Avoid foods containing the amino acid arginine, such as chocolate, cereal grains, nuts, and seeds.

● Eat plenty of red pepper as the capsaicin in this vegetable can block pain signals from nerves just under the skin.

● Liquorice contains several antiviral and immune-boosting components so either eat as a confection or drink a liquorice tea.

STRESS

Stress is rather a general term that is difficult to define. Stress is a normal part of everyday life to many people and at reasonable levels is not unhealthy. In fact most people need a certain amount of stress to keep them motivated; it is only when stress gets out of control that it becomes a problem. Our bodies are clever at coping with stress levels, but if they escalate to such a degree, then nervous exhaustion can hit us and we can become seriously ill. Finding out what triggers stress and discovering different ways of managing it is very important for us to enjoy life to the full.

● Diet and exercise are important in managing stress.

● Snack on celery and eat plenty of lettuce.

● Eat plenty of cherries as they can soothe the nervous system.

● Take a soothing bath in baking soda and ginger.

● Eat plenty of oats as they produce a calming effect.

● Choose pasta as a late night snack as it increases the brain chemical serotonin which has a calming effect on the body.

Chapter Eight

First Aid

Cuts and Grazes

I had a cut upon my knee
So ran to granny to see
If she could fix it straight away
'Cos I wanted to go back to play
Granny prodded it with her stick
And said a few herbs should do the trick

Cuts and grazes are a part of growing up, and I don't remember a day that I didn't have some sort of a scab on my knee or elbow. I was a tomboy through and through and loved nothing better than to climb trees, make precarious bridges across the brook, and take risks on my rather basic roller skates. The wheels were never round and as soon as I hit the smallest stone, down I went, arguing again with the paving stones. Summer holidays were always spent with granny and she was the one I always ran to when I had blood trickling down my legs or the sun had burnt the back of my neck. No sunscreen for us, just a blob of aloe vera gel to soothe the stinging and then back out to play with a handkerchief hanging out the back of my cap to protect my neck from further sunburn.

Granny always gave us a packed lunch tied up in an old piece of muslin. I remember the crusty bread, the piece of cheese, slice of home-cured ham, and an apple for afters. Amidst this rare feast was always a piece of homemade soap – not to wash our hands but just in case any of us kids got stung by a wasp or bee. She told us to wet it in the brook and then rub it on the sting to make the pain go away. Thankfully I never had to use it, but Johnny, our friend from down the road, was jolly thankful when he got stung on the ear.

BITES AND STINGS

We can get bites and stings from any number of insects, most of which cause little more than a mild discomfort. However, some people are allergic to stings so if you see someone have a violent reaction, or they have been stung in the mouth, seek medical help immediately. There are quite a few simple home remedies to minimize the pain and most of them work very quickly. Some insects, for example bees, leave the sting behind in the skin, and this should be removed carefully first before treating. It is best to get someone to try and flick it out using the blade of a knife rather than a pair of tweezers, because you don't want to squeeze the poison sac and send more toxins into your blood.

Treatment for bites and stings

● Put crushed ice in a plastic bag and apply it to the sting to reduce inflammation and itching.

● Any vinegar applied to a sting will make the pain a thing of the past. Either use it neat or mix it with bicarbonate of soda to make a paste and apply it to the area of the sting.

● Apply neat lemon juice to the sting.

● Stinging insects seem to be repulsed by the odour of garlic, so eat plenty in your diet and it should keep the little blighters at bay.

● Rub a piece of raw onion on the bite to minimize infection and swelling.

● Rub basil leaves over your skin to act as an insect repellant. It works for Africans and Indians, who swear by it.

- Lemon grass is very similar to the lemon-scented plant citronella, which is used in many proprietary insect repellants. Crush the stem of the lemon grass and rub it over your skin.

BRUISES

Those black and blue marks that we get after we knock ourselves are caused by blood leaking out of the capillaries just under our skin. If the skin is not broken then there is no risk of infection, but they can still be very sore and unsightly so any help is welcome. Bruises are more common in elderly people due to the fact that their skin gets thinner with age.

Treatment for bruises

- Apply an icepack to the bruise to reduce pain and swelling, particularly if the bruise is associated with a sprain. A day later, apply a heat pad to the affected area to dilate the blood vessels and improve circulation.

- Arnica is a herb with pain-relieving, antiseptic, and anti-inflammatory properties. Only use externally and make a healing solution by using one teaspoon of the dried herb to a cup of boiling water. Allow to cool sufficiently before applying.

- Apply apple cider vinegar and cold water to the bruise.

- Soak a bandage in comfrey tea and apply to the bruised area.

- Crush some parsley leaves and apply to the bruise; the marks should subside within a couple of days.

- Apply a piece of raw potato to the bruise or eat some fresh pineapple as it contains enzymes that promote healing.

BURNS

If you have a severe burn then you must seek medical attention straight away, but if you have a mild first-degree burn that injures only the outermost layer of the skin then try some of the following treatments. Make sure you cool the burned area as quickly as possible under cold running water or apply some ice cubes. Remember, though, the old wives' tale about putting butter on a burn is a no-no, as anything fatty will literally fry the skin and make the burn worse.

Treatment for burns

- Aloe vera has been used for burns since the beginning of time. The gel from the plant takes the sting out of the burn almost immediately, reduces the risk of infection, and lessens the risk of scarring. No one should be without an aloe vera plant on their kitchen windowsill.

- Echinacea is not only great at building up the immune system, if used as a tincture it will quickly soothe the burn and help prevent infection.

- Apply a poultice of garlic and onion directly to the burn and leave on the skin until the burning sensation dies down.

- Lavender oil is great for soothing the pain and ensuring that the burn does not leave a scar.

- Wet clean gauze with a witch hazel decoction and bind it to the scalded or burned area.

- Cut up a raw potato, wet it, and hold it on the burn. This will help to draw out the heat.

CUTS AND GRAZES

Most cuts and grazes are minor and can easily be treated at home. However, if your injury is more severe and requires stitches, you will need to receive treatment in hospital. Make sure your hands are clean before treating any open wounds and ensure that there are no pieces of grit or dirt left in the cut or graze before treating. You can wash the area with distilled witch hazel or some warm water with a couple of drops of tea tree oil added. It might sting for a little while, but its antiseptic properties will help to heal the wound. After treatment make sure you cover the wound with a clean dressing to stop it from becoming infected.

Treatment for cuts and grazes

- Apply honey to the affected area as it has been proved to accelerate healing.

- Arnica is useful for treating and disinfecting wounds.

- Calendula tea can be used to rinse the wound as it is a potent antiseptic and healer.

- If you are having trouble stopping the bleeding, this treatment might sound a bit harsh but it does stem the flow. Sprinkle crushed black peppercorns into the wound as they curb excessive bleeding and have antibiotic properties as well.

- If you cut your finger outdoors and have nowhere to wash the wound, take a tip from our canine friends and lick the cut. Saliva has strong antiseptic properties.

FAINTING

Smelling salts (or sal volatile) were always carried by Victorian ladies in case they came over faint – which was very common in those days, probably due to their over-tight corsets. They are a combination of ammonium carbonate and perfume and the strong smell often brought the frail 19th-century women out of their faint. Today, no one carries around a bottle of smelling salts, but something similar would be handy. Fainting, or swooning, is simply a sudden loss of consciousness due to a decreased flow of blood to the brain. It can be caused by many things – hunger, exhaustion, severe heat or cold, emotional upset or pain, or a very stuffy environment. Either get the patient to put their head between their knees or get them to lie on their back and elevate their legs. This is to encourage the flow of blood back into the brain.

Treatment for fainting

● Drink coffee with a little cardamom added to stimulate the nervous system. If you prefer, hot chocolate works just as well as it contains caffeine.

● If you are prone to fainting, carry a little bottle of lavender oil in your bag so that you can use it to soak a handkerchief and inhale when needed.

● Eucalyptus is as close as you can get to modern-day smelling salts, so you might like to keep some of the oil handy.

● If you have a kettle to hand, brew up some rosemary tea and get the person to sip some to bring the colour back to their cheeks.

NOSEBLEEDS

Nosebleeds can be quite common in children and are a result of the rupture of small blood vessels in the nostrils, sometimes as a result of a knock or when the nostrils become dry in cold or hot conditions. Do not lay the patient on their back as this will cause the blood to run down their throat, which is not pleasant. Simply put a cold compress on the back of the patient's neck and then pinch the soft part of the nose firmly between the thumb and forefinger for several minutes. Then soak a pad of cotton wool in cold or iced water with a couple of drops of lemon oil or apple cider vinegar added. Place it firmly across the bridge of the nose or place a small plug up the nostril to speed up clotting. Remember, do not let the patient blow their nose, otherwise they will dislodge the clot and start the bleeding all over again.

SPRAINS AND STRAINS

A strain is an injury to the muscles and is usually caused by a sudden change in direction or lifting heavy weights and normally affects the neck, ankles, wrists or knees. A sprain is an injury affecting a joint, with the tendons that attach muscles to the bones being overstretched and sometimes torn. The first treatment is to put a cold compress or ice pack on the affected area for fifteen to twenty minutes and repeat every two to three hours to minimize the pain. The patient must rest and the injured part should be elevated to reduce the swelling.

Treatment for sprains and strains

- Arnica is the first remedy to consider in cases of sprains and strains. Applied externally it can alleviate pain and causes the reabsorption of blood that accumulates in the soft tissues when blood vessels are broken in an accident.

- Use lavender or chamomile oil in some iced water as a compress.

- Get the patient to include plenty of fresh pineapple in their diet as it contains bromelin which speeds up the healing process.

INDEX